SQUEEZE WORDS HARD

Maureen Alcorn
Amanda Ebborn

Longman

This book is dedicated to Adu.

'Sometimes, like you, I ponder
The many tomorrows before me...'

This book is illustrated by the following:

Jenny Beck, pages 10 and 22; Michael Hingley, pages 55
and 68–9; Andrew Laws, page 74; Patricia Moffett, pages
118–19, 181, 184–5 and 192; Mark Paulding, pages 37,
100 and 104–5; Clyde Pearson, pages 152–3 and 200;
Lynette Pitzolu, pages 114–15, 142–3 and 188; Grace
Richmond, pages 7 and 139; Emma Sutherland, pages 30,
97 and 158–9; Michael Whitehead, pages 60–1; Merida
Woodford, pages 64–5 and 154.

Headings by Kathy Baxendale on pages 60, 68, 74, 100,
105 and 158.

Cover illustration by Cathie Felstead.

contents

Generations apart 55

What's it like out there? 97

Nine to five 139

Waiting for the bell 181

introduction

There's nothing quite like poetry. In order to fully communicate their ideas and feelings in just a few lines, poets have to make words work really hard. That's why we've called this anthology '*Squeeze Words Hard*'. It's a phrase that's worth remembering as you read through the poems, because the more **you** squeeze the words, the more they'll have to say to you.

When you have selected the poems you like best, you will find a variety of things to do with them. There are opportunities to discuss, perform, compare, analyse and use the poems as a starting point for language work. You will discover that poetry is not only fun to read, but it can make you think about the world outside your doorstep and the people who live in it. The pupils we teach have enjoyed these poems – we hope you will too.

If I didn't laugh, I'd cry

How many times have you laughed at someone else's misfortune? We all enjoy a good laugh, but sometimes the things we choose to laugh at are not funny at all. So – why do we laugh? If we took everything too seriously, the world would be an unbearable place. In these poems, you might be surprised to find some serious topics treated in a lighthearted way. Each of the poets has obviously decided: 'If I didn't laugh, I'd cry'.

■ *Don't Interrupt!*

Turn the television down!
None of your cheek!
Sit down!
Shut up!
Don't make a fool of yourself!
Respect your elders!
I can't put up with you anymore!
Go outside.
Don't walk so fast!
Don't run.
Don't forget to brush your teeth!
Don't forget to polish your shoes!
Don't slam the door!
Have manners!
Don't interrupt when I'm talking!
Put your hand over your mouth when you cough.
Don't talk with your mouth full!
Go to the market with me.
You spend too much money!
No more pocket money for you dear.
Go to your room!
Don't stuff yourself with sweets!
Don't point!
Don't go too near the television.
You are not coming out until you have tidied your room.
Don't interrupt when I'm talking!

Did you get any homework today?
Always carry a pen to school.
Eat your dinner up.
Wear your school uniform!
Turn the television over to watch 'Dallas'.
Bring any letters home from school.
Come straight home tomorrow.
Tidy your bed.
Don't shout!
Don't listen to my conversation.
Don't look at the sun it could blind you.
Don't bite your nails!
Don't suck your thumb!
Why don't you answer me!
You never listen to a word I say!
Don't interrupt when I'm talking!

Demetroulla Vassili

Sat in the pub
Drink flowing free
Everyone's merry
Cept poor old me
I'm starving

I have to sit
in the corner
All quiet
The trouble you see
I'm on a diet
I'm starving

No whisky, no gin
Why did I come in
no ploughman's lunch
like that greedy bunch
I'm starving

Shall I walk to the bar
I won't go too far
Just a pkt of crisps
and one drink
I'm starving

Then I think I'll have
when I've finished this fag
some chicken and chips
in a basket
I'm starving

No I can't keep quiet
I'll shout, Bugger the diet
I'm absolutely starving

Maureen Burge

One Day in a Supermarket

Me have to check
    Everything
        One
    By one
    By one

No way me can spend
    The same money
    That me spend last month
    This month

Or we bound fe land up
    Out a door
    When me can't pay the rent

We bound fe plunge into darkness
    When them cut off the light

Me corn and bunion bound fe rebel
    Or me drop down dead
    With tiredness
When me have fe walk it
    Go a work this month

Food
  Is still
  The most
  Important though

But
    Me have to check everything
    One
    By one
    By one

No salt fish
    No salt mackerel
    No bully beef
    No milk powder

Only five pound pack
    A flour
    and sugar
At evergreen prices
    Two little soup bone
    Batter with dry season
One wingy chicken

What you say cashier
    God almighty
One hundred and thirtyfive dollars!
    And more cheeng!
    Cheeng! Cheeng!
Going up and up
Pon de Cash Register

Staap
    But this thing serious!

Elean Thomas ▨

▪ *Gutter Press*

News Editor: Peer Confesses,
                Bishop Undresses,
                Torso Wrapped in Rug,
                Girl Guide Throttled,
                Baronet Bottled,
                J. P. Goes to Jug.

      But yesterday's story's
      Old and hoary.
      Never mind who got hurt.
      No use grieving,
      Let's get weaving.
      What's the latest dirt?

    Diplomat Spotted,
    Scout Garrotted,
    Thigh Discovered in Bog,
    Wrecks Off Barmouth,

    Sex In Yarmouth
    Woman In Love With Dog,
    Eminent Hostess Shoots Her Guests,
    Harrogate Lovebird Builds Two Nests.

Cameraman: Builds two nests?
              Shall I get a picture of the lovebird singing?
              Shall I get a picture of her pretty little eggs?
              Shall I get a picture of her babies?

News Editor: *No!*
              Go and get a picture of her legs.

              Beast Slays Beauty,
              Priest Flays Cutie,
              Cupboard Shows Tell-Tale Stain,
              Mate Drugs Purser,
              Dean Hugs Bursar,
              Mayor Binds Wife With Chain,
              Elderly Monkey Marries For Money,
              Jilted Junky Says 'I Want My Honey'.

Cameraman: 'Want my honey?'
              Shall I get a picture of the pollen flying?
              Shall I get a picture of the golden dust?
              Shall I get a picture of a queen bee?

News Editor: *No!*
              Go and get a picture of her bust.

              Judge Gets Frisky,
              Nun Drinks Whisky,
              Baby Found Burnt in Cot,
              Show Girl Beaten,
              Duke Leaves Eton –

Cameraman: Newspaper Man Gets Shot!
              May all things clean
              And fresh and green
              Have mercy upon your soul,
              Consider yourself paid
              By the hole my bullet made –

News Editor: (dying) *Come and get a picture of the hole.*

Paul Dehn

The Telephone Call

They asked me 'Are you sitting down?
Right? This is Universal Lotteries'
they said. 'You've won the top prize,
the Ultra-super Global Special.
What would you do with a million pounds?
Or, actually, it's more than a million –
not that it makes a lot of difference
once you're a millionaire.' And they laughed.

'Are you OK?' they asked – Still there?
Come on, now, tell us, how does it feel?'
I said 'I just . . . I can't believe it!'
They said 'That's what they all say.
What else? Go on, tell us about it.'
I said 'I feel the top of my head
has floated off, out through the window,
revolving like a flying saucer.'

'That's unusual' they said. 'Go on.'
I said 'I'm finding it hard to talk.
My throat's gone dry, my nose is tingling.
I think I'm going to sneeze – or cry.'
'That's right' they said, 'don't be ashamed
of giving way to your emotions.
It isn't every day you hear
you're going to get a million pounds.

Relax, now, have a little cry;
we'll give you a moment . . .' 'Hang on!' I said.
'I haven't bought a lottery ticket
for years and years. And what did you say
the company's called?' They laughed again.
'Not to worry about a ticket.
We're Universal. We operate
a Retrospective Chances Module.

Nearly everyone's bought a ticket
in some lottery or another,
once at least. We buy up the files,
feed the names into our computer,
and see who the lucky person is.'
'Well, that's incredible' I said.
'It's marvellous. I still can't quite . . .
I'll believe it when I see the cheque.'

'Oh', they said, 'there's no cheque.'
'But the money?' 'We don't deal in money.
Experiences are what we deal in.
You've had a great experience, right?
Exciting? Something you'll remember?
That's your prize. So congratulations
from all of us at Universal.
Have a nice day!' And the line went dead.

Fleur Adcock ▨

Telephone Conversation

The price seemed reasonable, location
Indifferent. The landlady swore she lived
Off premises. Nothing remained
But self-confession. 'Madam', I warned,
'I hate a wasted journey – I am African.'
Silence. Silenced transmission of
Pressurised good-breeding. Voice, when it came,
Lipstick coated, long gold-rolled
Cigarette-holder pipped. Caught I was, foully.
'HOW DARK?' . . . I had not misheard . . . 'ARE YOU LIGHT
OR VERY DARK?' Button B. Button A. Stench
Of rancid breath of public hide-and-speak.
Red booth. Red pillar-box. Red double-tiered
Omnibus squelching tar. It *was* real! Shamed
By ill-mannered silence, surrender
Pushed dumbfounded to beg simplification.
Considerate she was, varying the emphasis –
'ARE YOU DARK? OR VERY LIGHT?' Revelation came.
'You mean – like plain or milk chocolate?'
Her assent was clinical, crushing in its light
Impersonality. Rapidly, wave-length adjusted,
I chose. 'West African sepia' – and as afterthought
'Down in my passport.' Silence for spectroscopic
Flight of fancy, till truthfulness clanged her accent
Hard on the mouthpiece. 'WHAT'S THAT?' conceding
'DON'T KNOW WHAT THAT IS.' 'Like brunette.'
'THAT'S DARK, ISN'T IT?' 'Not altogether.
Facially, I am brunette, but madam, you should see
The rest of me. Palm of my hand, soles of my feet
Are a peroxide blonde. Friction, caused –
Foolishly madam – by sitting down, has turned
My bottom raven black – One moment madam!' – sensing
Her receiver rearing on the thunderclap
About my ears – 'Madam,' I pleaded, 'wouldn't you rather
See for yourself?'

Wole Soyinka

The Class Game

How can you tell what class I'm from?
I can talk posh like some
With an 'Olly in me mouth
Down me nose, wear an 'at not a scarf
With me second-hand clothes.
So why do you always wince when you hear
Me say 'Tara' to me 'Ma' instead of 'Bye Mummy dear'?
How can you tell what class I'm from?
'Cos we live in a corpy, not like some
In a pretty little semi, out Wirral way
And commute into Liverpool by train each day?
Or did I drop my unemployment card
Sitting on your patio (We have a yard)?
How can you tell what class I'm from?
Have I a label on me head, and another on me bum?
Or is it because my hands are stained with toil?
Instead of soft lily-white with perfume and oil?
Don't I crook me little finger when I drink me tea
Say toilet instead of bog when I want to pee?
Why do you care what class I'm from?
Does it stick in your gullet like a sour plum?
Well, mate! A cleaner is me mother
A docker is me brother
Bread pudding is wet nelly
And me stomach is me belly
And I'm proud of the class that I come from.

Mary Casey

Colonisation in Reverse

Wat a joyful news, Miss Mattie,
I feel like me heart gwine burs'
Jamaica people colonizin
Englan in reverse.

By de hundred, by de t'ousan
From country and from town,
By de ship-load, by de plane-load
Jamaica is Englan boun.

Dem a-pour out o' Jamaica,
Everybody future plan
Is fe get a big-time job
An settle in de mother lan.

What a islan! What a people!
Man an woman, old and young
Jusa pack dem bag an baggage
An tun history upside dung!

Some people don't like travel,
But fe show dem loyalty
Dem all a-open up cheap-fare-
To-Englan agency.

An week by week dem shippin off
Dem countryman like fire,
Fe immigrate an populate
De seat o' de Empire.

Oonoo see how life is funny,
Oonoo see de tunabout,
Jamaica live fe box bread
Outa English people mout'.

For wen dem catch a Englan,
An start play dem different role,
Some will settle down to work
An some will settle fe de dole.

Jane say de dole is not too bad
Bacause dey payin she
Two pounds a week fe seek a job
Dat suit her dignity.

Me say Jane will never find work
At the rate how she dah look,
For all she stay pon Aunt Fan couch
An read love-story book.

Wat a devilment a Englan!
Dem face war an brave de worse,
But I'm wonderin how dem gwine stan
Colonizin in reverse.

Louise Bennett

I had rather be a woman
Than an earwig
But there's not much in it sometimes.
We both crawl out of bed
But there the likeness ends.
Earwigs don't have to
Feed their children,
Feed the cat,
Feed the rabbits,
Feed the dishwasher.
They don't need
Clean sheets,
Clean clothes,
Clean carpets,
A clean bill of health.
They just rummage about
In chrysanthemums.
No one expects them
To have their
Teetotal, vegetarian
Mothers-in-law
To stay for Christmas,
Or to feel a secret thrill
At the thought of extending the kitchen.
Earwigs can snap their pincers at life
And scurry about being quite irresponsible.
They enjoy an undeserved reputation
Which frightens the boldest child.
Next time I feel hysterical
I'll bite a hole in a dahlia.

Daphne Schiller

■ *Men Are*

Men are, men are, men are.
men are strong
men are tough
men are surly, men are rough
men have mates
men drink beer
men are brave and don't show fear
men slap backs
men sing songs
men are men and men are strong
men don't touch
men aren't drips
men shake hands with vice-like grips.

men like fighting
men like cars
men like shouting with men in bars
men like football
and now and then
men like men like men like men
no they don't
men beat up queers
men live with their mums for years and years
men have beards
and hairy chests
men walk through blizzards in string vests.

men can embrace
and bare their soul
but only if they've scored a goal
men leap tall buildings
men are tough
men don't know when they've had enough
men drive fast cars with wide wheels
men like fur-lined steering wheels
men have muscles
men have sweat
men haven't learnt to grow up yet.

men wear trousers
men have flies
men kick sand in each other's eyes
men stand alone
men show no fears
men have hobbies and hairy ears
men have willies
men have bums
men are good at science and sums
men aren't loving
men don't dance
men don't change their underpants.

men climb mountains
in the snow
men don't cook and men don't sew
men are bosses
men are chums
men build office blocks and slums
men make bombs
men make wars
men are stupid, men are bores
men ignore
what women see
and call our story **his**tory.

The Joeys

▨ *I Wouldn't Thank You for a Valentine* *(Rap)*

I wouldn't thank you for a Valentine.
I won't wake up early wondering if the postman's been.
Should 10 red-padded satin hearts arrive with sticky sickly saccharine
Sentiments in very vulgar verses I wouldn't wonder if you meant them.
Two dozen anonymous Interflora roses?
I'd not bother to swither over who sent them!
I wouldn't thank you for a Valentine.

Scrawl SWALK across the envelope
I'd just say 'Same Auld Story
I canny be bothered deciphering it –
I'm up to here with Amore!
The whole Valentine's Day Thing is trivial and commercial.
A cue for unleasing cliches and candyheart motifs to which I
    personally am not partial.'
Take more than singing Telegrams, or pints of Chanel Five, or sweets,
To get me ordering oysters or ironing my black satin sheets.
I wouldn't thank you for a Valentine.

If you sent me a solitaire and promises solemn.
Took out an ad in the Guardian Personal Column
Saying something very soppy such as 'Who Loves Ya, Poo?
I'll tell you, I do, Fozzy Bear, that's who!'
You'd entirely fail to charm me, in fact I'd detest it
I wouldn't be eighteen again for anything, I'm glad I'm past it.
I wouldn't thank you for a Valentine.

If you sent me a single orchid, or a pair of Janet Reger's in a
    heartshaped box and declared your Love Eternal
I'd say I'd not be caught dead in them they were politically suspect and
    I'd rather something thermal.
If you hired a plane and blazed our love in a banner across the skies;
If you bought me something flimsy in a flatteringly wrong size;
If you sent me a postcard with three Xs and told me how you felt
I wouldn't thank you, I'd melt.

Liz Lochhead ▨

Ballad of the Landlord

Landlord, landlord,
My roof has sprung a leak.
Don't you 'member I told you about it
Way last week?

Landlord, landlord,
These steps is broken down.
When you come up yourself
It's a wonder you don't fall down.

Ten bucks you say I owe you?
Ten bucks you say is due?
Well, that's ten bucks more'n I'll pay you
Till you fix this house up new.

What? You gonna get eviction orders?
You gonna cut off my heat?
You gonna take my furniture and
Throw it in the street?

Um-huh! You talking high and mighty.
Talk on – till you get through.
You ain't gonna be able to say a word
If I land my fist on you.

Police! Police!
Come and get this man!
He's trying to ruin the government
And overturn the land!

Copper's whistle!
Patrol bell!
Arrest.

Precinct station.
Iron cell.
Headlines in press:
Man threatens landlord
Tenant held no bail
Judge gives Negro 90 days in county jail

Langston Hughes

Insec' Lesson

Todder nite mi a watch one program,
Yuh did watch it to Miss Vie?
De one wid de whole heap o' ants an' bug,
Mi couldn' believe mi yeye

When mi see ow de ants dem lib
An hep out one anedda,
So much hundred tousan ants
Dey wuk an' pull togedda.

De mooma ants she big an fat
So she liddung lay egg all day.
De solja ants tan up guard de door,
Mek sure no enemy no come dem way.

De worka ants a de bessis one,
Dem always wuk togedda
Fi feed de queen, an store de eggs,
An wash dem likkle bredda.

Some go out fi gadda food
Fi feed dose in de nes'
Some a dig hole fi mek new room
An some clean up de mess.

I' please mi fi see ow de ants dem pull,
An try fi get tings done,
Dem wuk an eat an sleep togedda
An a not even dem one.

Far mi see whole heap o' odda insect
Wasp, bug an fly an bee,
All a wuk togedda,
Ina perfec' harmony.

Dat couldn' happen a fi mi yahd,
Ivy woulda nebba wash Tim,
An Joe would mus dead fi hungry
If a Amos fi fine food fi 'im.

But uman-been fool-fool yuh know,
Look ow wi fight an cuss,
Steada wi lib in unity like de ants,
Wi lib like dawg an puss.

De man sey a because o' unity
Mek de ants dem still aroun,
If we no unite, animals might soon start reign
Wid mankind six feet undergroun'.

Valerie Bloom ▨

POLITICS

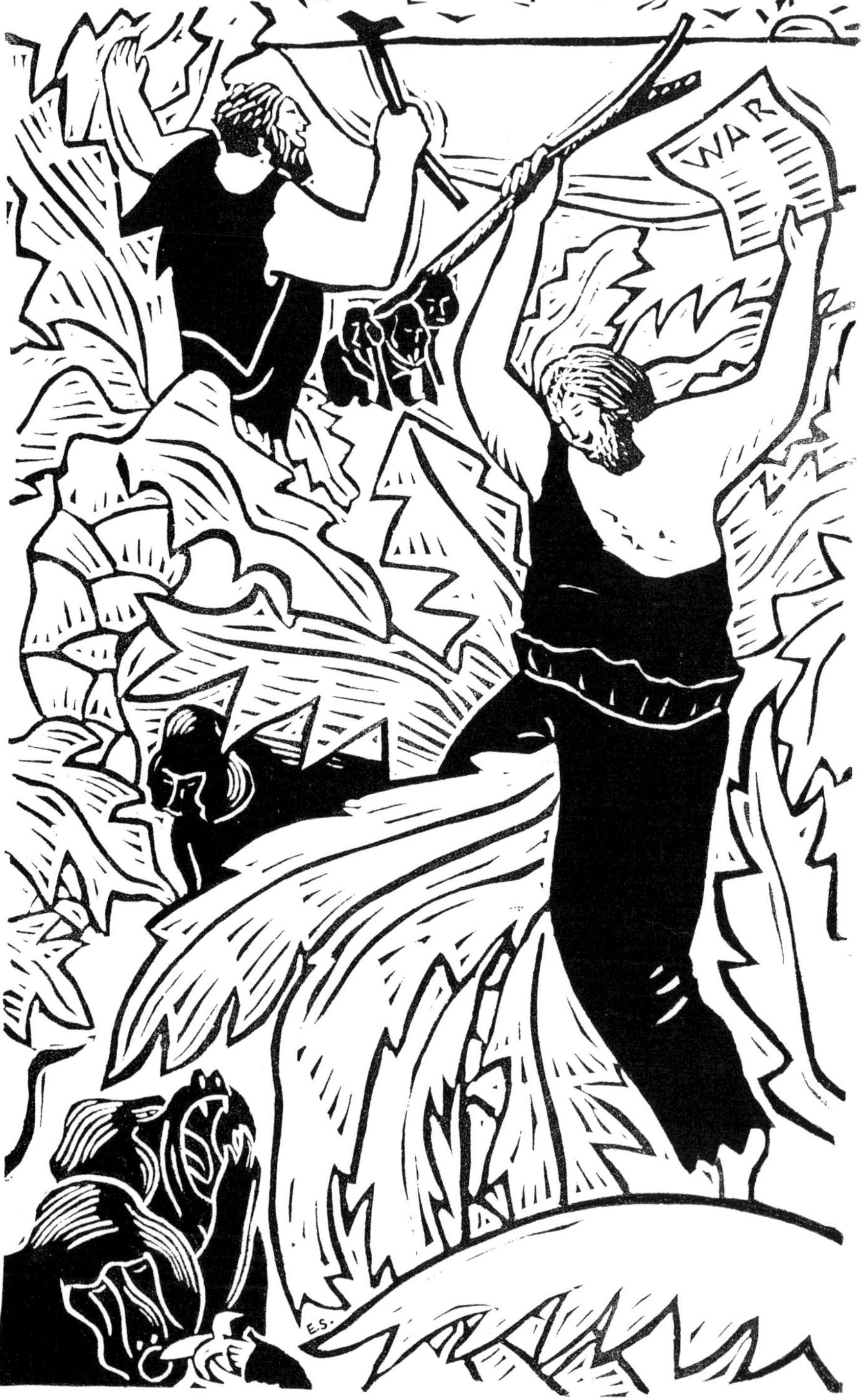

One day, two men were shipwrecked
    On an Island far away.
They hardly knew each other, so
    There wasn't much to say.

By the time a week had passed,
    The two were rather bored;
And so they went their separate ways
    Each of his own accord.

Yes, separate lives for different men;
    This answer seemed the best.
One lived on the Eastern side;
    The other, to the West.

After a month, a problem emerged;
    How could they bide their time?
There was nothing here to buy
    And neither had a dime.

So they turned to politics
    (After all, here they were free.)
Each ruled over a herd of baboons
    And governed from a tree.

One was a Fascist dictator;
    The other, a Democrat.
But both held absolute power
    And did all they could with that.

Four year plans were developed;
    Troops were armed and trained.
(The baboons, by the way, did little but eat
    And they all ran away when it rained.)

Borders were drawn out and settled.
    Pacts were written and signed.
Trade was begun and a currency too,
    Nuclear bombs were designed.

Everything flourished and went very well,
  But soon the two found it a bore.
They planned a few interesting terrorist attacks
  And said that the answer was war.

The baboons, by this time, had begun to be cross
  And gathered throughout the wood,
Wondering why they were all getting bombed
  For the so-called 'common good'.

Armed with bananas, they crept up behind
  A major official tree.
At one baboon's shout, the two men stepped out,
  After which both were thrown in the sea.

Once they were wet, they both saw the folly
  Of what they had done out of greed.
But sure enough, one week later,
  Neither had paid any heed.

They swam to another island,
  Vowing that peace was best.
But nevertheless, one headed for East
  While the other decided on West.

Sarah Goossens

Icarus Allsorts

'A meteorite is reported to have landed
in New England. No damage is said...'

A littlebit of heaven fell
From out the sky one day
It landed in the ocean
Not so very far away
The General at the radar screen
Rubbed his hands with glee
And grinning pressed the button
That started World War Three.

From every corner of the earth
Bombs began to fly
There were even missile jams
No traffic lights in the sky
In the time it takes to blow your nose
The people fell, the mushrooms rose

'House!' cried the fatlady
As the bingohall moved to various parts
of the town

'Raus!' cried the German butcher
as his shop came tumbling down

Philip was in the countinghouse
Counting out his money
The Queen was in the parlour
Eating bread and honey
When through the window
Flew a bomb
And made them go all funny

(By the way if you're wondering
What happened to the maid
Well in this particular raid
She lost more than her nose
In fact she came to a close
Or so the story goes.)

In the time it takes to draw a breath
Or eat a toadstool, instant death.

The rich
Huddled outside the doors of their fallout shelters
Like drunken carolsingers

The poor
Clutching shattered televisions
And last week's editions of T.V. Times
(but the very last)

Civil defence volunteers
With their tin hats in one hand
And their heads in the other

CND supporters
Their ban the bomb mojos beginning to rust
Have scrawled 'I told you so' in the dust.

A littlebit of heaven fell
From out the sky one day
It landed in Vermont
North-Eastern U.S.A.
The general at the radar screen
He should have got the sack
But that wouldn't bring
Three thousand million, seven hundred,
    and sixty-eight people back,
Would it?

Roger McGough

■ *In Westminster Abbey*

Let me take this other glove off
    As the *vox humana* swells,
And the beauteous fields of Eden
    Bask beneath the Abbey bells.
Here, where England's statesmen lie,
Listen to a lady's cry.

Gracious Lord, oh bomb the Germans.
    Spare their women for Thy Sake,
And if that is not too easy
    We will pardon Thy Mistake.
But gracious Lord, whate'er shall be,
Don't let anyone bomb me.

Keep our Empire undismembered
    Guide our Forces by Thy Hand,
Gallant blacks from far Jamaica,
    Honduras and Togoland;
Protect them Lord in all their fights,
And, even more, protect the whites.

Think of what our Nation stands for,
    Books from Boots' and country lanes,
Free speech, free passes, class distinction,
    Democracy and proper drains.
Lord, put beneath Thy special care
One-eighty-nine Cadogan Square.

Although, dear Lord, I am a sinner,
    I have done no major crime;
Now I'll come to Evening Service
    Whensoever I have the time.
So, Lord, reserve for me a crown,
And do not let my shares go down.

I will labour for Thy Kingdom,
  Help our lads to win the war,
Send white feathers to the cowards
  Join the Women's Army Corps,
Then wash the Steps around Thy Throne
In the Eternal Safety Zone.

Now I feel a little better,
  What a treat to hear Thy Word,
Where the bones of leading statesmen,
  Have so often been interr'd.
And now, dear Lord, I cannot wait
Because I have a luncheon date.

John Betjeman

The President's Visit

The President visited us today,
his face a beaming china chamber-pot.
The male nurses had changed the sheets before
he came. The floor was swept of bandages
that had collected there with bits of skin —
what with the casualties piling in hard
even the sweepers have been asked to help
the surgeons. Anyway, the President
came, smiling, of course, and walked down the row
of beds. He walked slowly, naturally,
and his words foamed at his mouth like lather
collected round a leak in a drain-pipe.
He took hours reaching my bed and paused
frequently by others, raising a hand
like a dog raises his leg by a lamp-post,
a sort of blessing, you see, bestowed
on the bleeding soldiers. I must say though,
between you and me, mind, he looked something
like a bull with his snout of a mouth

as he wandered among the gored matadors
of his Republic's army. I wanted
to talk to him but he was such a haystack
of a loaded camel through the needle-eye
of this ward, so ponderously weighed
by the burden of his official visit,
that I thought a donkey can't be as slow,
and I was dangling the carrot of my
broken arm at him, too, not being able
to wave. Hell, I thought, the others have just
wounds, maybe one or two with fractured skulls
and one shot in a place I'm sure
the President wouldn't be shown – then
an awful thing happened. My weak bladder
is no secret, and as he approached me
it grew worse. Damn it, I thought, if he raises
his hand at me and I think of that dog
again, this bed will turn to a lamp-post.
This thought just about deflated
the bloated opulence of his visit
which had glowed so benignly in this ward
like a setting sun. My lavatory -
attendant's mind is my own undoing
at times, I was thinking when he reached
my bed. And what was I supposed to do then?
Hold his porcelain ears like the handles
of a chamber-pot and piss in his face?
It isn't easy with a broken arm.

Zulfikar Ghose ▨

oral work

Here are some suggestions of activities arising from the poems which involve talking, listening, discussing and even performing. Some of these ideas might lead to written assignments, but that is up to you and your teacher.

performing poems

It is always better to hear a poem than just to read it, but some poems are best when performed. To perform a poem in a group, you need to consider the following points:

■ How many 'parts' could you make? How can the poem be divided up into different voices?

■ Think like a performer. How should people say the lines? Are any actions, sound effects or props needed?

■ You will need to rehearse. Should people learn their lines? Everyone will need a copy of the poem so they know which is their part.

If you take all these points into consideration, your poem should come to life.

The following poems are ideal for performance. You will probably find others which work too. A good size for a group is four people. After the performance, get into groups to discuss how it went. Ideas are provided for further discussion on each poem.

■ *Don't Interrupt!* *by Demetroulla Vassili*

To start

Each person in the group reads the poem to themselves, then listens to one member of the group reading it out loud. Now work through these points:

1 How many people could be speaking in this poem? Try to divide the poem into sections, e.g. groups of lines start with the word 'Don't'.

2 When you have made your divisions, decide which lines each member of the family would say. You could have a mother, father and perhaps an older brother or sister.

3 If the poem is read in the same loud tone from beginning to end, it loses its effect. Decide on the tone and volume of your different sections in the poem: some lines could be performed sarcastically or wearily or enquiringly.

4 Are there any lines which could be said altogether as a group?

When you have had your discussions and made your decisions, you are ready to start rehearsing.

After the performance

Do you think the poem represents a realistic picture of family life? During your performance, the rest of the class probably laughed. Why do you think they did this? What is funny about the poem? Discuss what the members of your group get told off for at home.

■ *One Day in a Supermarket* *by Elean Thomas*

This poem is best performed by two or three people.

To start

Each person in the group reads the poem to themselves, then listens to one member of the group reading it out loud. Now work through these points:

1 Is the speaker in the poem a man or a woman? Does it make any difference?

2 How old do you think the speaker is and what is their role in the family?

3 What is the speaker's attitude towards rising prices? Is it angry, resigned, irritable, challenging? Is the attitude the same throughout the poem or does it change?

4 How would you say the last line?

5 The poem is written in dialect. Try saying part of it in standard English. What's the difference? Which is more successful and why?

6 Can you work out what the word 'fe' means?

7 How can you divide the poem up and what actions could you use? Will someone take the part of the cash register?

8 Despite its serious message, the poem is humorous. How will you put this humour across?

When you have had your discussions and made your decisions, you are ready to start rehearsing.

After the performance

The person in the poem is struggling to afford the most basic kinds of food. Discuss and make a list of what the group considers are the most important items for families to buy every week. Which food items in your house could your family really do without (e.g. biscuits, crisps)?

The speaker in the poem considers food to be the 'most important' thing to spend money on. Do you agree?

▨ *Gutter Press*   *by Paul Dehn*

To start

Each person in the group reads the poem to themselves, then listens to one member of the group reading it out loud. Now work through these points:

1 Make sure you understand the meaning of all the words in the poem. This is vital if you are to bring out the humour in your performance.

2 What does the title mean? Is it appropriate? Which daily newspapers does it apply to?

3 What kind of man is the news editor? Is he likeable?
What kind of man is the cameraman?
Who do you like best, and how will you show the difference between them in your performance?

4 Think carefully about how you can divide up the poem. Are there sections which could be performed by the whole group?

5 What tone of voice will you use for the headlines? Will it change? Does the same person have to read them all?

6 Whose 'side' do you think the poet is on – the news editor's or the cameraman's?

When you have had your discussions and made your decisions, you are ready to start rehearsing.

After the performance

Discuss what elements a story has to have to be suitable for a headline in the gutter press. What are the different categories? Make a list. Think of five current news stories and write two headlines for each story – one suitable for a television bulletin or 'quality' newspaper, the other suitable for the gutter press.

The Telephone Call by Fleur Adcock

This poem is best performed by three people – the narrator, the representative from Universal Lotteries and the customer.

To start

Each person in the group reads the poem to themselves, then listens to one member of the group reading it out loud. Now work through these points:

1 Find out what a 'lottery' is and the meaning of the term 'Retrospective Chances Module'.

2 Decide which lines will be performed by which character.

3 What tone would the representative use? Would it change during the course of the poem?

4 Look at the 'customer's' reactions and experiment with the different ways they could be expressed, e.g. joyfully, excitedly, disbelievingly.

5 What the narrator says is important because it provides the links between the conversation. Think carefully about how these 'links' should be performed.

6 How can you most effectively bring out the contrast between the two sentences which form the last line of the poem?

When you have had your discussions and made your decisions, you are ready to start rehearsing.

After the performance

Discuss what point you think Fleur Adcock is trying to make in this poem. The last verse will help you to understand why Universal Lotteries made the call. A large number of companies now try to sell their products by phoning people in their homes, sending out leaflets or knocking on their doors. Discuss whether you think this is an effective way of selling things and if it is fair on the public. In particular, you need to think about the vulnerability of certain groups within society, such as the old and the easily led.

Men Are   *by The Joeys*

(The Joeys were an alternative cabaret act composed of four men who wrote this poem for performance on stage.)

To start

Each person in the group reads the poem to themselves, then listens to one member of the group reading it out loud. Now work through these points:

1 How can the poem best be divided up between members of the group? Are there any parts which could be said together?

2 Most of the lines begin with the word 'men', which sets up a definite beat to the poem. See if you can reflect this in your performance.

3 Much of the humour in this poem can be brought out by actions. Which will you include?

4 At the beginning, the poem appears to be written in praise of men, but by the end, it is obviously critical of them. Where does the change in tone occur and how will you make it clear in your performance?

5 In the last six lines, the Joeys make their point very forcefully. Discuss how these lines should be performed. In particular look at the emphasis on the last word of the poem and discuss its pronunciation.

When you have had your discussions and made your decisions, you are ready to start rehearsing.

After the performance

Are The Joeys describing all men in their poem? Is it a fair portrayal? Let each member of the group choose three statements from the poem which best describe what they think men 'are'. Discuss your choices and try to arrive at a consensus.

Telephone Conversation   *by Wole Soyinka*

This poem is best performed by three people – a narrator, the caller and the landlady.

To start

Each person in the group reads the poem to themselves, then listens to one member of the group reading it out loud. Now work through these points:

1 . Some of the vocabulary and images used in the poem are difficult. Look up any words you don't know and discuss the meaning of the images.

2 Decide which lines the landlady says and find clues in the poem which will indicate her accent and tone.

3 Identify the lines which the man says out loud to the landlady on the telephone. What tone will you use and will it change? Are there any pointers in the poem which will help you to decide?

4 The narrator expresses the caller's thoughts. How should these lines be performed?

When you have had your discussions and made your decisions, you are ready to start rehearsing.

After the performance

The landlady's first question is 'How dark?' Why should she ask this and what possible difference could it make to her final decision? Why doesn't the landlady want the African in her property? This poem was written over twenty years ago. How have things changed?

other suggestions for oral work

1 | What makes us laugh?

The poems in this section, although about serious topics, are often written in a lighthearted way. No doubt some of them amused you – but why? Your task is to conduct a survey in your class to find out what makes people laugh.

a In your group, decide on a list of suitable questions to ask. You could divide the survey into different areas of humour, e.g. TV programmes, comedy acts, films, real-life situations.

b Look carefully at the answers you get and see if the group can spot any sort of pattern emerging.

c Report your findings to the class.

2 | A ten-minute lesson

Working by yourself or in pairs, choose your favourite poem from this section. How could you present it to the rest of the class? Your task is to give a ten-minute lesson using the poem either by itself or with other materials, in a way which will keep the class interested and involved.

3 | Role play

The following suggestions for role play are for pairs. The ideas in the poems will help you get started. Choose one or two of these role plays.

The Telephone Call by Fleur Adcock

Imagine you are the customer who received the call from Universal Lotteries. After you have recovered from the shock of this telephone conversation, you are very angry about the experience they have put you through. You decide to ring back and speak your mind. Role play this situation.

Telephone Conversation by Wole Soyinka

The poem ends with the words 'wouldn't you rather see for yourself?' Role play the conversation which might take place between the two characters at the landlady's home, leading to the acceptance of him as a tenant.

Don't Interrupt! by Demetroulla Vassili

In this poem, a young person is obviously being told off for things she has said and done. In your pair, role play a similar conversation between a young person in trouble with either a parent or a teacher, using some of the ideas from the poem. Make sure you use the phrase 'Don't interrupt' at least once.

The President's Visit by Zulfikar Ghose

This poem is about a politician visiting a hospital to see men wounded in war. In your pair, role play a visit by a famous person of your choice to a patient in a hospital ward.

4 A talk to the class

The poets in this section share an ability to see humour in situations where we don't usually expect to find it. You probably know someone who can describe the most ordinary event in an amusing way. Your task is to choose one of the following topics and present a talk to the rest of the class which is designed to make them laugh.

■ Job interviews, a visit to the dentist, exams, hobbies, pets, Saturday jobs, politics and growing up.

5 So what are the issues?

In your group, go through every poem in the section and decide exactly what issue is being tackled by the poet. Try to arrive at one sentence for each poem which sums up the poet's message.

written work

The written work has been divided into two sections: Language assignments and Literature assignments. Within each section, there are opportunities to write in a variety of ways about the poems you have read. The range of written work is designed to meet the requirements of whichever GCSE examination course you are doing. Your teacher will help you to select the right assignments for you and your course.

language assignments

1

The poem 'Don't Interrupt' highlights many of the sources of arguments between young people and their parents or teachers. In this assignment you are going to do some research into the subject. There are three stages:

Research

Design a questionnaire that you can use with pupils in your year to find out what causes their parents and teachers to moan at them. Begin by writing out a checklist of statements that pupils could either agree or disagree with. This could be followed by more detailed questions. Aim to question at least twenty pupils so that you can see a pattern developing. This completed questionnaire will form the first part of your assignment.

Interviews

You are going to do three separate interviews with a pupil, a parent and a teacher. The aim is to ask questions that will give them the opportunity to discuss what they find annoying about each other! If they agree, use a tape-recorder so that it will be easier to write up the interviews afterwards.
Think carefully about the questions you are going to ask. Interviewing someone else's parents and people in your year you don't know very well will probably be most useful because you won't already know their views.
Write up your three interviews in the same way you would set out a play – names in the margin and no speech marks.

Presenting your findings

You should be prepared to record your findings in several different ways: e.g. statistics or percentages from your questionnaire; extracts from your interviews; and your own opinions and conclusions.

Present your findings either:

a as a written speech you could give to the class; or
b as a newsheet or article for your school magazine.

2 Choose a title from one of the poems in the section and use it as a starting point for a story.

3 Playwriting

Here are suggestions for plays you can write, based on a range of situations described in some of the poems in this section.

Your play should start with a cast list, include details of where each scene is set and have clear stage directions. Put the characters' names in the margin and don't use speech marks.

Choose *one* of the following situations:

a An argument which involves all members of a family. The starting point could be something quite trivial, such as which TV programme to watch or a noisy stereo. Show how the argument develops and how it is finally resolved. This will probably involve several scenes if the argument continues into the following day.

b Two friends discussing their worries about a third friend's sudden weight loss. This scene should be followed by a second where all three characters discuss the dangers of over-dieting. Try to bring out the conflict between the dieter and the friends.

c Conversations at a supermarket check-out involving staff and/or customers. This does not have to take the form of an argument about prices or payment; it could be a conversation between customers in the queue or two check-out assistants.

d A group of friends plotting to play a Valentine's trick on someone, perhaps a classmate or a teacher. You could also include the follow-up scene, showing whether the trick succeeded or failed.

4 Many thought-provoking issues are raised by the poems in this section. This assignment gives you the opportunity to say what you think about some of them. Though individual poems could act as a starting point, it is up to you to do some research on your chosen topic before you begin your final essay. This could take the form of interviewing a range of people who could provide facts and opinions; checking a variety of newspapers for recent stories and using your school and local libraries. Television and radio programmes can also be a useful source of information. Research is necessary so that your opinions can be supported by facts and examples:

The problems and pressures of being either over or under weight.
The importance of social class in relation to quality of life and future prospects.
The morality of the 'gutter press'.
The changing role of men and women in our society.
The greatest problems in the world today are caused by men.
In war, no one wins.
The importance/relevance of religion in Britain today.
Never trust a politician.
Racism and how to tackle it.

These are not titles, they are areas for research which your teacher will help you to explore in order to form the basis of an assignment. Your own title will grow out of your research.

5 Wouldn't life be interesting if we could change the outcome of things we've said or done in the past, just like the Retrospective Chances Module offered in the poem 'The Telephone Call'. For this assignment write a story about someone for whom this becomes a reality. If you prefer, you could write about real events from your own life.

6 The following lines are taken from poems in this section. Choose one of the lines and use it as either the first or last sentence of a story.

'Don't make a fool of yourself!'
'What was I supposed to do?'
'Come on now, tell us, how does it feel?'
'Never mind who got hurt'

literature assignments

1   'Don't Interrupt', 'The Diet', 'One Day in a Supermarket', 'I Had Rather be a Woman', 'Ballad of the Landlord'

Choose *three* of the above poems. For each poem, write the letter you think the character might send to a magazine problem page outlining their problems. You should try to cover at least one side of A4 paper for each letter. When you have written all three letters, finish the assignment with a paragraph explaining which of the characters you sympathise with most and why.

2   **a** Choose the three poems which in your opinion best reflect the title of this section, 'If I Didn't Laugh, I'd Cry.' Carefully explain your choice and refer closely to the poems.

      b Do you think it is appropriate to use humour when you are making a serious point? Give your reasons, using any of the poems in this section to support your argument.

3   Choose two poems from this section – one you liked and one you didn't. Write a letter to each of the poets explaining in detail the reasons for your response. Justify your comments by referring closely to each of the poems. Each letter should cover at least a side and a half of A4 paper.

4   It's not only what people say but the way that they say it that's important, and this is particularly true of the poems in this section. For this assignment you have to interview the main characters described in *two* of the following poems. In order to set out your interviews clearly, invent names for the characters and put these in the margin along with your name as the interviewer. Aim to ask each character at least four questions: carefully prepare these questions so that the answers can be as full and detailed as possible. You should base your questions and answers on the details given in the poems.

Gutter Press by Paul Dehn

In this interview, you question the cameraman after he has just shot the news editor. You should bring out how he felt about his job and his reasons for shooting his boss.

The Class Game by Mary Casey

In this interview you need to bring out what the character thinks is the difference in language and lifestyle between the working class and the middle class. You should also show what she feels about this.

I Had Rather be a Woman by Daphne Schiller

In this interview, you need to question the character about the problems she faces as a wife and mother. Include some details about the tasks she has to do and bring out her feelings of frustration.

5 Choose three to five poems from this section and say why you liked them.

6 Many of the poems in this section are either by women or written from a woman's perspective. In what ways do you think this is significant?

7 Telephone Conversation by Wole Soyinka

Write a critical appreciation of this poem. Addressing the following points will help you:

■ In the poem, the choice of words and images and the way they are listed and ordered is unusual, e.g.

> '... Voice, when it came,
> Lipstick coated, long gold-rolled
> Cigarette-holder pipped. Caught I was, foully'.

Look carefully at Soyinka's use of language and show how it contributes to your understanding of: the landlady's character; the caller's character; the atmosphere created by the surroundings.

■ How would you describe and illustrate the humour in this poem?

■ The conversation between the two turns into a conflict of wills. Show how this develops and decide who really wins in the end.

■ Why has Soyinka chosen the format of a telephone conversation to make his point about racism?

51

8   Colonisation in Reverse by Louise Bennett

Read the poem carefully and complete all three following sections.

a The tone of this poem is mischievous. Comment on how the style, rhythm and use of creole (dialect) contribute to this. It might help to rewrite some verses in standard English so that you can appreciate the effectiveness of the original.

b Bring out the irony in the title of this poem.

c Miss Mattie never replies to the speaker in this poem. Your task in this section is to add three to five verses to the original, inserting them wherever it seems appropriate. Each verse should keep to the rhythm and style of Louise Bennett's poem, and should express Miss Mattie's views about emigrating to England, their mutual friend Jane or how the English are going to react to colonisation in reverse.

9   Men Are by The Joeys and I Wouldn't Thank You for a Valentine by Liz Lochhead

You have been asked to present these two poems to the rest of the class. As any teacher will tell you, preparation is important. In this assignment you have to cover all aspects of the two poems necessary for the class to get maximum understanding and enjoyment from them.
It will help you if you consider the following points:

■   Are there any words or phrases in the poems which pupils might not be familiar with? Make a list and give clear definitions.
The poems deal with male and female stereotypes. Look at the image the poets have chosen to use and discuss how effective they are. Do not make a list. Write about the messages each poet is giving and draw on the images to support your points.

■   Each poem ends with a twist. What effect does this have?

■   Both of these poems have been written for performance. How does this affect their style and rhythm? Are there any similarities or differences here? Is one more successful than the other? Give your reasons.

When you finally write up your assignment, remember that although it is divided into sections, you should not present it in note form but as a continuous piece of writing.

10 Men Are by The Joeys

a Write a letter to the Joeys telling them what you liked about their poem. At the end of the letter, invite them to your school to give a performance.

b Write your own poem in the same style as 'Men Are' which you could perform for the Joeys. Your title can be either 'Kids Are' or 'Teachers Are'.

11

Your local Council has organised an Arts Week which will include a day on the enjoyment and understanding of poetry. The audience will consist of pupils, teachers, poets and interested members of the public. You have been asked to write a speech for this occasion comparing and contrasting the two poems 'Insec' Lesson' and 'Politics'. Your task is to show how, in their very different ways, both poems are making the same point. Members of the audience will have copies of the poems, so you should refer directly to specific lines or phrases.

12 Icarus Allsorts by Roger McGough

a Write a critical appreciation of the poem. Addressing the following points will help you.

■ In the context of nuclear war, what do you understand by the terms 'mushrooms', 'civil defence volunteers' and 'CND supporters'?

■ In the first verse, the General pushes the button which starts the third world war. What has caused him to make this decision? (It would help to look at the first two lines.) Secondly, what does the use of the words 'glee' and 'grinning' tell you about the General?

■ McGough makes it clear that in the case of a nuclear attack, no one would survive. Which individuals and groups of people has he chosen to include in the poem? What is significant about the images associated with their different reactions?

■ Why have the CND supporters scrawled 'I told you so' in the dust?

■ Why does McGough end the poem with a question?

■ Nuclear war poses the most serious threat known to our world. Why then has McGough chosen as his format a cheerful rhyming style with the inclusion of a traditional children's nursery rhyme?

■ Look at the title of this poem. Find out who Icarus was and what the connection could be between him and any of the characters in the poem. Why do you suppose McGough completed his title with the word 'Allsorts'? There may be several reasons for this.

b John Betjeman's poem 'Westminster Abbey' refers to the Second World War while 'Icarus Allsorts' anticipates the third. Bring out the similarities and differences between these two poems and show how each poet seems to have little faith in humanity.

13   Westminster Abbey by John Betjeman

Write a critical appreciation of this poem. Addressing the following points will help you.

■ Essential to your appreciation of the poem is an understanding of the following phrases: 'vox humana', 'beauteous fields of Eden', 'sent white feathers to the cowards' and 'the Eternal Safety Zone'

■ Look closely at verses 2, 3, and 4. What is the woman in the poem praying for? What is significant about her order of priorities?

■ Look at the details the woman selects in verse 4. What do they tell you about her background and attitudes?

■ Why is the woman offering up her prayer in Westminster Abbey? What do you suppose this place represents to her?

■ What is the woman prepared to offer God in return for Him answering her prayers?

■ How would you define the woman's view of God?

■ The last verse begins with the line 'Now I feel a little better'. What does this indicate about her motives for prayer?

■ By the end of the poem, the reader is left in no doubt about Betjeman's view of the woman. How has he built up this impression? What particular techniques in language and style has he employed?

14

With close reference to 'Westminster Abbey' by John Betjeman and 'The President's Visit' by Zulfikar Ghose, show how both these poems deal with the theme of hypocrisy.

15   The President's Visit by Zulfikar Ghose

In TV news items, we often see politicians or members of the Royal Family visiting victims of disasters, and we assume that those visited are grateful for the attentions bestowed on them. Zulfikar Ghose shows another side to one such visit and makes us question the visitor's motives. Show how he manages to achieve this effect in his poem.

Generations apart

Growing up can be a tricky business whatever age you are. You may think life gets easier as you grow older, but be warned – there are many hurdles along the way! The poems in this section explore many different views about growing old, how some fight against it and others enjoy it. There are also poems about the relationship between young and old: a few manage to bridge the generation gap while others remain 'generations apart'.

▧ *Grandad*

When we go over
to my grandads
he falls asleep.

While he's asleep
he snores.

When he wakes up,
he says,
'Did I snore?
did I snore?
did I snore?'

Everybody says, 'No,
you didn't snore.'

Why do we lie to him?

Michael Rosen ▧

▧ *Sunday Afternoon in the Lounge of an Old People's Home and Monday Morning in Class with 4X*

Alf and Stanley,
Charlie and Flo,
Maud and Eliza,
Betty and Joe
Sit in a circle
Smelling of age
Muttering, mumbling,
Chewing on rage.

Exploding bubble gum
Hooking out bogeys,
Don't give a toss
For yesterday's fogeys.
But Jason, Gary,
Tracey and Dawn,
It's for you they're keeping
Those lounge seats warm.

Robert Bush

Crabbed Age and Youth

Crabbed Age and Youth
Cannot live together:
Youth is full of pleasance,
Age is full of care;
Youth like summer morn,
Age like winter weather;
Youth like summer brave,
Age like winter bare.
Youth is full of sport,
Age's breath is short;
Youth is nimble, Age is lame;
Youth is hot and bold,
Age is weak, and cold;
Youth is wild, and Age is tame.
Age, I do abhor thee;
Youth, I do adore thee;
O, my Love, my Love is young!
Age, I do defy thee:
O, sweet shepherd, hie thee!
For methinks thou stay'st too long.

William Shakespeare

Hugger Mugger

I'd sooner be
Jumped and thumped and dumped,

I'd sooner be
Slugged and mugged... than **hugged**...

And clobbered with a slobbering
Kiss by my Auntie Jean:

You know what I mean:

Whenever she comes to stay,
You know you're bound

To get one.
A quick
  short
  peck
  would
  be
  OK.
But this is a
Whacking great
Smacking great
Wet one!

All whoosh and spit
And crunch and squeeze
And '**Dear** little boy!'
And 'Auntie's missed you!'
And 'Come to Auntie, she
Hasn't **kissed** you!'
Please don't do it, Auntie,
PLEASE!

Or if you've absolutely
Got to,

And nothing on **earth** *can persuade you*
Not to,

The trick
Is to make it
Quick*,*

You know what I mean?

For as things are,
I really would far,

Far sooner be
Jumped and thumped and dumped,

I'd sooner be
Slugged and mugged . . . than **hugged** *. . .*

And clobbered with a slobbering
Kiss *by my Auntie*

Jean!

__Kit Wright__ ▨

On Ageing

When you see me sitting quietly,
Like a sack left on the shelf,
Don't think I need your chattering,
I'm listening to myself.
Hold! Stop! Don't pity me!
Hold! Stop your sympathy!
Understanding if you got it,
Otherwise I'll do without it!

When my bones are stiff and aching
And my feet won't climb the stairs,
I will only ask one favour:
Don't bring me no rocking chair.

When you see me walking, stumbling,
Don't study and get it wrong.
'Cause tired don't mean lazy
And every goodbye ain't gone.
I'm the same person I was back then,
A little less hair, a little less chin,
A lot less lungs and much less wind,
But ain't I lucky I can still breathe in.

Maya Angelou

The Family

She arrives home with a problem,
Needing time to think.
Mother and father, grey and old,
Kiss her.
She walks in,
Expensive clothes
Strong odour of French perfume
Whilst the parents cling to their drab grey world
And the tired apartment.
The parents, grateful for the time she's given them,
Forget when all their time was hers,
No appreciation for their used-up bodies
Given away for her.
She may realise there is no reason to feel guilty,
But she just doesn't have the time.
The people who gave her all their time and energy
Have become a butt for her jokes.
She meant to phone, but . . .
Or write, only . . .
But anyhow, she's home now,
So what's the difference?
They're only her parents
But she outgrew them long ago;
She outgrew them,
So why does she need to make excuses?
Because she loves them,
and after all, they are her parents . . .

Jenny Fromer

◼ *Son Dream*

I went looking for my son
and found him in the grass,
prone, his chin in his hands,
watching a black bull snake.
I said, 'Be careful, my son,
anything can happen.'
Beside him, somehow, a possum
rolled from under leaves, bared its teeth
but licked his ear. I said
'Watch out.' At that
a coon appeared,
touched my son's nose
gently with its pink fingers,
and lay down beside him.
I stood in my tracks, afraid, until
a wolf rose from the grass,
and licked my son's forehead.
My heart pumped the word 'rabid'
into the space behind my eyes.
'He is only twelve, Lord,' I prayed.
The gun was soundless when I fired.
The snake, the animals
began to shine, to shine.
My son and I walked home, holding hands.
He said, 'I love you,'
but when I looked back he lay in the grass,
his chin cupped in his hands,
the snake and animals a shining
circle around him.

William Heyen ◼

NETTLES

My son aged three fell in the nettle bed.
'Bed' seemed a curious name for those green spears,
That regiment of spite behind the shed:
It was no place for rest. With sobs and tears
The boy came seeking comfort and I saw
White blisters beaded on his tender skin.
We soothed him till his pain was not so raw.
At last he offered us a watery grin,
And then I took my billhook, honed the blade
And went outside and slashed in fury with it
Till not a nettle in that fierce parade
Stood upright anymore. And then I lit
A funeral pyre to burn the fallen dead,
But in two weeks the busy sun and rain
Had called up tall recruits behind the shed:
My son would often feel sharp wounds again.

Vernon Scannell

■ *Poem to My Daughter*

'I think I'm going to have it,'
I said, joking between pains.
The midwife rolled competent
sleeves over corpulent milky arms.
'Dear, you never have it,
we deliver it.'
A judgement years proved true.
Certainly I've never had you

as you still have me, Caroline.
Why does a mother need a daughter?
Heart's needle – hostage to fortune –
freedom's end. Yet nothing's more perfect
than that bleating, razor-shaped cry
that delivers a mother to her baby.
The bloodcord snaps that held
their sphere together. The child,
tiny and alone, creates the mother.

A woman's life is her own
until it is taken away
by a first particular cry.
Then she is not alone
but a part of the premises
of everything there is.
A branch, a tide . . . a war.
When we belong to the world
we become what we are.

Anne Stevenson ■

Lies

Telling lies to the young is wrong.
Proving to them that lies are true is wrong.
Telling them that God's in his heaven
And all's well with the world is wrong.
The young know what you mean. The young are people.
Tell them the difficulties can't be counted,
and let them see not only what will be
but see with clarity these present times.
Say obstacles exist they must encounter
Sorrow happens, hardship happens.
The hell with it. Who never knew
The price of happiness will not be happy.
Forgive no error you recognise,
it will repeat itself, increase,
And afterwards our pupils
will not forgive in us what we forgave.

Y. Yevtushenko

When I am an old woman I shall wear purple
With a red hat which doesn't go, and doesn't suit me,
And I shall spend my pension on brandy and summer gloves
And satin sandals, and say we've no money for butter.
I shall sit down on the pavement when I'm tired
And gobble up samples in shops and press alarm bells
And run my stick along the public railings
And make up for the sobriety of my youth.
I shall go out in my slippers in the rain
And pick the flowers in other people's gardens
And learn to spit.

You can wear terrible shirts and grow more fat
And eat three pounds of sausages at a go
Or only bread and pickle for a week
And hoard pens and pencils and beermats and things in boxes.

But now we must have clothes that keep us dry
And pay our rent and not swear in the street
And set a good example for the children.
We will have friends to dinner and read the papers.
But maybe I ought to practise a little now?
So people who know me are not too shocked and surprised
When suddenly I am old and start to wear purple.

Jenny Joseph

■ *Note for the Future*

When I get old
don't dress me in
frayed jackets
and too-short trousers,
and send me out
to sit around bowling-greens
in summer.
Don't give me just enough
to exist on, and expect me
to like passing
the winter days
in the reading-room
of the local library, waiting
my turn to read
last night's local paper.
Shoot me!
Find a reason, any reason,
say I'm a troublemaker,
or can't take care of myself
and live in a dirty room.
If you're afraid
of justifying my execution
on those terms,
tell everyone I leer
at little girls, and then
shoot me!
I don't care why you do it,
but do it,
and don't leave me
to walk to corner-shops
counting my coppers,
or give me a pass to travel cheap
at certain times, like a leper.
Don't send me to a home
to sit and talk
about the weather.

I don't want free tours,
half-price afternoon film-shows,
and friendly visitors.
If I can't live in independence
get me when I'm sixty-five, and
shoot me, you bastards, shoot me!

Jim Burns ▩

Maple Syrup

August, goldenrod blowing. We walk
into the graveyard, to find
my grandfather's grave. Ten years ago
I came here last, bringing
marigolds from the round garden
outside the kitchen.
I didn't know you then.
                              We walk
among carved names that go with photographs
on top of the piano at the farm:
Keneston, Wells, Fowler, Batchelder, Buck.
We pause at the new grave
of Grace Fenton, my grandfather's
sister. Last summer
we called on her at the nursing home,
eighty-seven, and nodding
in a blue housedress. We cannot find
my grandfather's grave.
                              Back at the house
where no one lives, we potter
and explore the back chamber
where everything comes to rest: spinning wheels,
pretty boxes, quilts,
bottles, books, albums of postcards.
Then with a flashlight we descend
firm steps to the root cellar – black,
cobwebby, huge,
with dirt floors and fieldstone walls,
and above the walls, holding the hewn
sills of the house, enormous
granite foundation stones.
Past the empty bins
for squash, apples, carrots, and potatoes,
we discover the shelves for canning, a few
pale pints
of tomato left, and – what
is this? – syrup, maple syrup

in a quart jar, syrup
my grandfather made twenty-five
years ago
for the last time.
                        I remember
coming to the farm in March
in sugaring time, as a small boy.
He carried the pails of sap, sixteen-quart
buckets, dangling from each end
of a wooden yoke
that lay across his shoulders, and emptied them
into a vat in the saphouse
where fire burned day and night
for a week.
                    Now the saphouse
tilts, nearly to the ground,
like someone exhausted
to the point of death, and next winter
when snow piles three feet thick
on the roofs of the cold farm,
the saphouse will shudder and slide
with the snow to the ground.
                                Today
we take my grandfather's last
quart of syrup
upstairs, holding it gingerly,
and we wash off twenty-five years
of dirt, and we pull
and pry the lid up, cutting the stiff,
dried rubber gasket, and dip our fingers
in, you and I both, and taste
the sweetness, you for the first time,
the sweetness preserved, of a dead man
in his own kitchen,
giving us
from his lost grave the gift of sweetness.

Donald Hall ▓

To a Crippled
Schoolmaster

We hogged the billiard table in your room,
We read your weekly *Mirrors* with delight,
Retailed your humorous pomposities
And roared with laughter at your sharp tongue's bite.

I still recall your dragging up the steps
And setting out some time before each bell;
I liked your funny classes (though in truth
I really cannot claim you taught us well).

Sadly we watched you grow from bad to worse,
Drag slower and slower until that summer term
You kept your room and classes came
To see you fade from ailing to infirm.

When you retired from teaching – as you had to,
When body couldn't serve your eager will –
We built a special house to cage you in
Where you could watch the football matches still.

Less often than I could I looked you up
And saw your living carcass wasting slow,
Your sprightliness of mind a crudish irony
When all your wretched limbs were withering so.

Without a conscious plan to be neglectful
I didn't seem to find the time
To drop in for your casual commentary
On what you called 'the national pantomime'.

I wonder whether time has stolen from me
Something that matters deeply (or should do)
And whether anything I manage now will ever
Quite kill my guilt about neglecting you.

And when you die I know I shall be sorry,
Remembering your kindness. But the fear
Of facing death stops me from coming
To see you dying smiling in your chair.

Mervyn Morris

The Strangers

The strangers have vanished –
Two, aged, inseparable Edwardians,
A lady and a gentleman,
Dated by their wardrobe.
They had lived behind hedges
And trees in a flint cottage
Untouched by t.v. and car.

They were seen occasionally
Walking slowly and elegantly
In the sun, a curious pair
In black from an album world
Of bible, lace and gramophone.
They retreated from our tinsel
World of prosperity, and we,
Their strangers, came in from
The city with children and car
To live in the country and disturb
A century of tranquillity.

I passed the flint cottage many times,
And passing glanced between two bars
Of a locked gate, (the only space
In a massive hedge spilling over
A flint wall bent by hungry roots),
A weed path led to the cottage
Wreathed in ivy, lichen and dust.

One summer day I climbed into the garden
Where a lawn, deep in seeding grass,
Was spreading four ways under the boughs
Of a great oak and beyond under sycamores
And sumacs statuelike and geometric
Against the sky. I felt the uninhabited
Stillness and the strange air of time past
Stirring in the quiet friction of foliage . . .
And I heard, from gaping windows, the cry
Of hollow rooms . . . The residue of human
Habitation lay scattered like leaves
Of a dozen Autumns, and an arch of roses
Hung like spirals of barbed wire.

Beyond this barrier I stood
In a darker region where the sun
Simmered behind a green canopy
With shafts of silver light.
A summer-house of shadows
And fungus lay trapped
In an arena of green time.
A tree, cut close to earth,
And a fallen, rustic table,
Were sinking into waves of grass.
They were requisites for tea
On the lawn – broken mirrors
For a glance at silhouettes.

I listened to the little sounds –
The interpreters of a derelict place
And over my shoulder four shattered
Rectangles, with ivy teeth, seemed like
A monster guarding a sanctuary
Of frozen reality . . . I retreated
And emerged at the road, drenched
By dark references of a lost age.

Robert Morgan

Dick Straightup

Past eighty, but never in eighty years –
Eighty winters on the windy ridge
Of England – has he buttoned his shirt or his jacket.
He sits in the bar-room seat he has been
Polishing with his backside sixty-odd years
Where nobody else sits. White is his head,
But his cheek high, hale as when he emptied
Every Saturday the twelve-pint tankard at a tilt,
Swallowed the whole serving of thirty eggs,
And banged the big bass drum for Heptonstall –
With a hundred other great works, still talked of.
Age has stiffened him, but not dazed or bent,
The blue eye has come clear of time:
At a single pint, now, his memory sips slowly,
His belly strong as a tree bole.

He survives among hills, nourished by stone and height.
The dust of Achilles and Cuchulain
Itches in the palms of scholars; thin clerks exercise
In their bed-sitters at midnight, and the meat salesman can
Loft fully four hundred pounds. But this one,
With no more application than sitting,
And drinking, and singing, fell in the sleet, late,
Dammed the pouring gutter; and slept there; and, throughout
A night searched by shouts and lamps, froze,
Grew to the road with welts of ice. He was chipped out at dawn
Warm as a pie and snoring.

The gossip of men younger by forty years –
Loud in his company since he no longer says much –
Empties, refills and empties their glasses.
Or their strenuous silence places the dominoes
(That are old as the house) into patterns
Gone with the game; the darts that glint to the dartboard
Pin no remarkable instant. The young men sitting
Taste their beer as by imitation,
Borrow their words as by impertinence
Because he sits there so full of legend and life
Quiet as a man alone.

He lives with sixty and seventy years ago,
And of everything he knows three quarters is in the grave,
Or tumbled down, or vanished. To be understood
His words must tug up the bottom-most stones of this village,
This clutter of blackstone gulleys, peeping curtains,
And a graveyard bigger and deeper than the village
That sways in the tide of wind and rain some fifty
Miles off the Irish sea.
                    The lamp above the pub-door
Wept yellow when he went out and the street
Of spinning darkness roared like a machine
As the wind applied itself. His upright walk,
His strong back, I commemorate now,
And his white blown head going out between a sky and an earth
That were bundled into placeless blackness, the one
Company of his mind.

Obit.

Now, you are strong as the earth you have entered.

This is a birthplace picture. Green into blue
The hills run deep and limpid. The weasel's
Berry-eyed red lock-head, gripping the dream
That holds good, goes lost in the heaved calm
Of the earth you have entered.

Ted Hughes

■ The Flower-Press

We bend over my old flower-press,
mother and young daughter,
you full of excitement and chatter,
me nervous as I open it
after its years of dust-gathering
on the shelf.
In here we discover
the fastened flowers,
the originals I remember placing
carefully between the sheets
of green blotting paper,
fragments to me now,
ghosts of flowers,
the pressure has been too great
for their lives to bear.
Dry, frail, faded,
each leaf, petal and frond;
I lay them one by one
on your own hand.
Gathered and preserved from the years
before you were born,
to me these flowers are flawed.
For me their place has been taken by you,
my own flower, ever-growing, changing.
Am I right to warn you of their imperfections?
Should I try to show you how lives may be grasped,
and like these flowers shut in, immobilized?
Or am I bringing you too soon word of corruption,
too much stillness?
No matter, for you are not listening.
With bright eyes you say,
'aren't they beautiful, can I press some too?'
Seeing only the beauty.
So like pure air reaching into areas
long since sealed off, now reclaimable,
you lead me forward without fear.
Deeper and deeper you draw me into life,
you make the dead come alive again
by sensing how even the shadow of a flower
may be perfect, and so suffice.

Penelope Shuttle ■

■ *oral work*

Here are some suggestions of activities arising from the poems which involve talking, listening, discussing and even performing. Some of these ideas might lead to written assignments, but that is up to you and your teacher.

performing poems

It is always better to hear a poem than just to read it, but some poems are best when performed. To perform a poem in a group, you need to consider the following points:

■ How many 'parts' could you make? How can the poem be divided up into different voices?

■ Think like a performer. How should people say the lines? Are any actions, sound effects or props needed?

■ You will need to rehearse. Should people learn their lines? Everyone will need a copy of the poem so they know which is their part.

If you take all these points into consideration, your poem should come to life.

The following poems are ideal for performance. You will probably find others which work too. A good size for a group is four people. After the performance, get into groups to discuss how it went. Ideas are provided for further discussion on each poem.

■ *Grandad*   by Michael Rosen and
Sunday Afternoon   by Robert Bush

Here we are asking you to perform *two* short poems. They include many opportunities for action and you must ensure that every group member contributes something towards one of the performances.

To start

Each person in the group reads the poems to themselves, then listens to one member of the group reading them out loud. Now work through these points:

Grandad

1 Choose someone to perform the part of grandad. They will have to decide how to say the lines 'Did I snore?' and exactly what sort of snore they'd like to do.

2 'No, you didn't snore' is said by everybody. How are you going to say this line? Practise different ways, e.g. loudly, jokingly, sarcastically, irritably.

3 Decide who is going to say the rest of the lines (it could be more than one person) and discuss in particular how the last line should be performed.

Sunday Afternoon

1 Discuss whose side you think the poet is on – the old or the young people's. Give your reasons.

2 There are twelve names mentioned in the poem. Your group will not have this many people, so think of some way you could use the rest of the class to help with your performance.

3 Using just your group members, decide how you are going to divide up the lines and the actions.

4 **a** Which words and phrases in the first verse tell you how the old people feel? How should these be performed?
  b What is the *attitude* of the young people in the second verse? Which words and phrases tell you this and how should these be performed?
  c Look very carefully at the last two lines. Do you think that there is a change of mood here? What is it, and how should these lines be performed so that they make their point?

When you have had your discussions and made your decisions, you are ready to start rehearsing.

After the performance

Why do the family in the first poem lie to grandad? Can you think of any examples from your own experience when you or your family have lied to an old person for similar reasons? Were you right to lie? In the second poem, the young people are lying to themselves. What are they lying about and why are they doing it?

▪ *Crabbed Age and Youth*   *by William Shakespeare*

This poem probably works best when performed by two or three people rather than a larger group.

To start

Each person in the group reads the poem to themselves, then listens to one member of the group reading it out loud. Now work through these points:

1 Find out the meanings of 'crabbed' and 'abhor'.

2 Shakespeare describes age as being 'crabbed'. How do the images (words used to describe age) bear this out?

3 How old do you think Shakespeare was when he wrote the poem and what is his attitude towards ageing?

4 **a** Make two columns. In one, write down the words and phrases used to describe youth, e.g. 'full of pleasance'. In the other, list the words and phrases used to describe age, e.g. 'full of care'.

  b Now you are going to play a game of 'verbal ping pong'! Get one person to read the first item on the 'youth list' and another to respond to the first item on the 'age list'. Work your way down to the bottom of each list and then discuss what *tone* was used by the readers. Try it again using different tones. For example, youth could be: boastful, mocking, cheerful, brisk, energetic, dismissive. Age could be: bitter, angry, sad, resigned, pathetic. (Look up any words you're not sure of.)

  Which tones or combinations seem to convey the meaning of the poem best?

  Now go back to the *full* poem and see how it works.

5 Look carefully at the last six lines.

    a 'Age, I do abhor... do defy thee'.

    Who will say these lines? Are they as straightforward as the earlier part of the poem where youth and age have clearly separate statements to make? Could the readers perhaps swop roles here? Discuss this.

    b Now look at the last two lines.

    Who is the 'sweet shepherd' and what does Shakespeare mean when he says 'thou stay'st too long'? Who are these lines directed towards? Can these lines be performed by the two people reading 'youth' and 'age'? How should they be said? What tone should be used?

When you have had your discussions and made your decisions, you are ready to start rehearsing.

After the performance

Shakespeare states that youth and age 'Cannot live together'. Should the generations cut themselves off from each other in this way? Talk about the effect this attitude can have on individuals, families and society as a whole.

▄ *Hugger Mugger*   *by Kit Wright*

To start

Each person in the group reads the poem to themselves, then listens to one member of the group reading it out loud. Now work through these points:

1 How old do you think the boy in the poem is and why?

2 How do you picture Auntie Jean? Do you have any relatives like her?

3 Do you like the title of the poem? Try to explain what is good about it.

4 Do you think the boy would *really* prefer to be 'Jumped and thumped and dumped' and 'slugged and mugged'? If not, why did he say so?

5   **a** Decide which lines Auntie Jean says.

    b How do the words in bold help you to perform these lines?

    c What actions could be used by the person performing the part of Auntie Jean?

6 Are there any lines in the poem the rest of the group could perform *together*?

7 Look at the lines which are left and decide how you want to divide up what the boy says to himself and to the reader. Do you want to include any actions?

When you have had your discussions and made your decisions, you are ready to start rehearsing.

After the performance

Do you think that the 'Hugger mugger' could have been an *uncle* rather than an aunt? Do boys and girls react differently to people showing them affection and if so, why? As a group, talk about your own relatives and how they greet you. Does it have any thing to do with their age or their closeness to the family?

Son Dream *by William Heyen*

To start

Each person in the group reads the poem to themselves, then listens to one member of the group reading it out loud. Now work through these points:

1 The poem is about a dream. What happens in the poem to make this clear?

2 Look at what the father says. Think carefully about how his lines should be said and who he is talking to.

3 Find out what a 'possum' and a 'coon' are. These two words indicate that the poem is written by an American. Experiment with reading the poem (or parts of it) in an American accent and discuss how you think this might help the effectiveness of the performance.

4 How do we know that the boy is not afraid of the animals? Why don't they hurt him? What is his father so frightened of?

5 After the father has fired his gun, the poet describes the animals beginning 'to shine, to shine'. Why do you think this phrase is repeated and why, at the end of the poem, should the animals be in 'a shining circle'?

6 Think carefully about how the poem can be divided up for performance. Is there an opportunity to use actions?

When you have had your discussions and made your decisions, you are ready to start rehearsing.

After the performance

What are the worries parents have about their children? How do these worries differ according to the age and sex of the child? The father in the poem expresses his fears in a dream – how do most parents show theirs?

▨ *Note for the Future*   *by Jim Burns*

To start

Each person in the group reads the poem to themselves, then listens to one member of the group reading it out loud. Now work through these points:

1 How old do you think the man is at the moment? Give your reasons.

2 Who do you think the man in the poem is talking to? Give your reasons.

3 If you had to divide the poem into *verses*, how many would you have and where would you make the divisions? (There is no correct answer.)

4 The man in the poem gives a long list of all the things he *doesn't* want to happen to him when he gets old. Look at them and discuss whether you think they are as bad as he does. What is it about them that the man finds unacceptable, to the point where he'd rather be shot?

5 The words 'shoot me' occur four times. Discuss how you think they should be said. Will you use the same tone each time? Is it a good idea to have one member of the group saying just these words?

6 Discuss how you can divide the poem up into parts for performance and particularly concentrate on the changes of mood or tone.

When you have had your discussions and made your decisions, you are ready to start rehearsing.

After the performance

Discuss how society treats old people. Talk about what facilities are or should be available and what role the family should play.

other suggestions for oral work

1 Working by yourself or in pairs, choose your favourite poem from this section. How could you present it to the rest of the class? Your task is to give a ten-minute lesson using the poem either by itself or with other materials, in a way which will keep the class interested and involved.

2 Several of the poems are about the problems of being a parent. There are some things all children are warned against, e.g. obvious sources of danger, such as traffic, heights, fire etc. Guidance is also given on learning right from wrong, e.g. not to steal, tell lies, hurt people etc. All this is vital, but what about more positive advice, i.e. things you *should* rather than shouldn't do.

Now you're nearly an adult, you are in a position to start giving advice to people younger than you. Discuss and decide on the *ten* most important pieces of advice you would pass on to a person about to enter their teens, to help them make a success of their lives and avoid some of the problems you might have encountered. Try to make the advice as *positive* as you can.

3 ## Role play

The following suggestions for role play are for pairs or small groups. The ideas in the poems will help you to get started. Choose one or two.

Sunday Afternoon by Robert Bush

What kind of conversation might the old people in the first verse be having? Take a character each and work out a convincing role play.

Warning by Jenny Joseph and Note for the Future by Jim Burns

After a careful reading of the details in each poem, work out a role play between the woman and the man, which brings out their different views on growing old.

The Family by Jenny Fromer

Work out the conversation between the three characters in this poem. Try to make clear the tension which exists within the family.

4 Think of some old people you know well. They might be members of your family, or neighbours, or in the local community. Select three with different personalities and outlooks on life as a basis for a talk to the rest of the class. You might like to include details of appearance, mannerisms, lifestyle and personal history.

5 **a** In your group, read the poem 'Note for the Future' where Jim Burns refers to some of the facilities offered to old age pensioners (OAPs), such as travel passes and half-price cinema tickets. If it were within your power to make life better for OAPs, what *five* things would you offer them?

b Swop your list with that of another group and see where their priorities lie.

c Finally, in co-operation with the other group, make *one* list of five from the combined ten suggestions.

It is possible for the whole class to end up with just one list of five. This is up to you and your teacher.

6 Time capsule

In groups, your task is to decide on which *ten* items you would put into a time capsule being launched into space or buried underground. The items must represent the activities and interests of your age group and show any future generation/alien being what it was like to be a teenager in the last part of the twentieth century.

■ *written work*

The written work has been divided into two sections: Language assignments and Literature assignments. Within each section, there are opportunities to write in a variety of ways about the poems you have read. The range of written work is designed to meet the requirements of whichever GCSE examination course you are doing. Your teacher will help you to select the right assignments for you and your course.

language assignments

1 The Generation Game

One of the most popular types of TV programme is the quiz show. Many years ago, there was a show called *The Generation Game*, but it had little to do with generations.

In this assignment, your task is to create a new show called *The Generation Game*, but this time it should appeal to and feature people of all generations. Once you have got your idea, you should do the following:

a Write a factual account of the game, its rules, its scoring system and types of prize to be won.

b Write a letter to the famous person you would like to see presenting the game. In this letter, you should include a *brief* outline of the show – just enough to interest them.

c Design a full page advertisement for the *TV* or *Radio Times*, announcing your new programme.

d Write the review which might appear in a national newspaper the morning after *The Generation Game*'s first screening.

2 Personal writing

In this assignment, you will need to think about your relationships and experiences with older people. Choose *one* of the titles.

What it is like being a daughter/son

Think about the contribution you make to family life and what you expect from it.

Lessons in life

Which older people have influenced you most? You may choose up to three. Describe those people, their characters and the ways in which they have influenced you.

Getting it wrong, getting it right

Write two contrasting pieces. The first should describe a disagreement you've had with an older person and the second should be about an occasion when co-operation with an older person led to something positive. You may use play form for one or both of the pieces if you wish.

3 John Lennon and Paul McCartney wrote a very cheerful song about old age called 'When I'm 64'. What kind of life do you think *you* will be living when you are this age? What are your hopes and fears for your long-term future? Write your own essay entitled 'When I'm 64'.

4 This assignment gives you the opportunity to say what you think about some of the issues associated with age and youth. Choose *one* of them:

a Medical science is now so advanced that it can keep people alive for longer than ever before. What are the advantages and disadvantages of this for the old people themselves, their families, support services and society as a whole?

b The poems 'Nettles', 'Son Dream' and 'Lies' all deal with the desire of parents to protect their children. To what extent is it possible to prevent young people from coming to any harm? Should they be left to experience life to the full, even though that may be dangerous or painful for them?

c This assignment requires you to write an essay exploring the way different cultures at different times have viewed the role of age and youth. For example, in the Victorian age, young children were expected to work a full day – now, you have to be sixteen. In some cultures, 'childhood' doesn't exist, and young children play a full role in family and working life and are often married before their teens. In this country, the law requires that you end your full-time employment at sixty or sixty-five and retire from playing an active role in society, whereas in other cultures, the older you are, the more your influence increases. These are just a few examples. Your research should cover a wide range of differences, and in conclusion, you should decide which system is of most benefit to both young and old, and if none of them are, create your own 'ideal' system.

d In this society, some fear old age, whereas others look forward to their retirement years. How could our society make old age an enjoyable and useful period for all? Consider the level of state benefits; the role of the family; medical and nursing facilities; opportunities for employment and society's attitudes towards old age.

e Equal opportunities is no longer an issue when you reach the age of sixty-five – or is it? Discuss in relation to race, sex and class.

5

a Working in a small group or with a partner, look carefully at a range of newspapers and examine what kind of news reports and articles are written about the old and the young. Collect a sample of these and discuss whether you can see a pattern emerging. Are only certain kinds of story reported? Can you divide them into categories? The first part of this assignment is to write at least a side of A4 paper on your findings.

b Most newspapers have a special page for young people, but none offer a page exclusively for the over-sixties. The second part of this assignment is to design and write such a page. You will be able to get some ideas from the poems, but better still, why not interview some over-sixties to find out exactly what they would like to read about?

6 **Creative writing**

a Choose a title from *one* of the poems in the collection and use it as the starting point for a story.

b Within the next hundred years, it is estimated that at least half of this country's population will be over sixty. Think carefully about the implications of this and write a story set in the future which deals with some aspect of this situation.

c The following statements come from a recent television documentary:

■ In Britain, more than half of hospital beds are taken up by the elderly.

■ In the USA, over a million people live in old people's homes.

■ In Britain, one quarter of women over forty-five look after a sick, elderly relative.

Your task is to write a short story or play set in a geriatric ward, an old people's home, or the home of a woman caring for an elderly relative.

d Write a story about a young person rebelling against a parent/parents. You could call this story 'Generations Apart'.

e Write a story in which a grandparent refuses to behave in the way that is expected of them (see the poem 'Warning') and instead adopts the lifestyle of a teenager. Make up your own humorous title for this piece.

literature assignments

1 Choose up to five poems from this section which you particularly enjoyed and say why you liked them.

2 Choose two poems from this section – one you liked and one you didn't. Write a letter to each of the poets explaining in detail the reasons for your response. Justify your comments by referring closely to each of the poems. Each letter should cover at least a side and a half of A4 paper.

3 If you could meet two or three of the characters described in any of the poems in this section, which would you choose and why? Write about a side and a half describing your meeting with each one. This may take the form of an interview in play form.

4 Many of the poems in this section show the generations in conflict. With close reference to at least three poems, show clearly how each poet has treated this theme.

5 ## Hugger Mugger by Kit Wright

This poem describes a young boy's worries about his Auntie Jean coming to visit. Read the poem carefully and complete the following three tasks:

a Write the conversation (in play form) that you think the boy might have with a friend at school, the day before Auntie Jean is due to arrive. It is clear from the poem how he feels, so make sure you include some of the details in your play.

b Write the diary entry you think Auntie Jean might make after visiting her nephew.

c The boy thinks of his Auntie Jean as a 'hugger mugger'. Do you think this is a good description? Is it a good title for the poem? Write a paragraph giving your reasons.

6   Crabbed Age and Youth by William Shakespeare, On Ageing by Maya Angelou and Note for the Future by Jim Burns

Discuss the different views expressed on the ageing process in these three poems. You should refer closely to choice of language, style and tone.

7   The Family by Jenny Fromer

a Write a short critical appreciation of this poem, covering at least a side and a half of A4 paper. You should include the following points: why has the girl come home; how does she feel about her parents; how is her life different from theirs and how do they view her visit? Refer closely to the poet's choice of words and the tone she has created in the poem.

b Write the conversation you think the daughter might have with her parents after her arrival. Try to bring out the idea from the poem that all three are pretending everything is fine and not saying what they really think.

Then, *either*: Write the conversation the daughter might have that evening on the telephone to a friend about being back in her parents' flat,

Or: What the parents may say to each other that night, when they are alone. These conversations can be written in play form.

8   Son Dream by William Heyen, Nettles by Vernon Scannell and Lies by Y. Yevtushenko

These poems deal with the same theme – the desire of parents to protect their children. With close reference to the poems, write about their similarities and differences.

9   Poem to My Daughter by Anne Stevenson

a In her poem Anne Stevenson asks: 'Why does a mother need a daughter?' What answers does she offer in the poem?

b Comment on the different views of parenthood explored in 'Poem to my Daughter', 'Son Dream' and 'The Family'.

10 Warning by Jenny Joseph

Read the poem carefully, and complete the following three tasks:

a You are a neighbour of the old woman who wears purple. You have noticed her strange behaviour and feel it is your duty to report it to the local Social Services, because you suspect she is unable to look after herself properly. Write the letter, including the detail only a neighbour would be aware of.

b You are the social worker dealing with the case. Write the report you would make after you have visited the woman herself and talked to other neighbours and local people.

c Finally, imagine you are the old woman. You are extremely angry that a social worker has visited. Write a letter of complaint to the Director of Social Services explaining why you behave in the way you do.

11 Warning by Jenny Joseph and Note for the Future by Jim Burns

a The characters in these two poems have different attitudes towards growing old. With close reference to the details in each of the poems, explain what these attitudes are.
Finally, say which poem you liked best and why.

b Write your own poem which begins with the words: 'When I grow old'. You should aim to write 20 to 30 lines.

12 Maple Syrup by Donald Hall and The Flower-Press by Penelope Shuttle

a The Flower-Press

'to me these flowers are flawed.'
'With bright eyes you say,
' "aren't they beautiful ..." '
Explore the different reactions of the mother and daughter to the experience of looking at the flower-press. What does the poet suggest the mother learns from the daughter?

b Both these poems have a similar effect on the reader. They focus on the theme of continuity between the generations and the linking of past, present and future. With close reference to tone, choice of language and imagery in the poems, bring out the similarities.

13   Maple Syrup by Donald Hall

■   The poem tells a story. What is it?

■   The poem is divided into six verses. Look carefully at the divisions and see if you can provide each verse with a title which sums up its content.

■   The poem contains a good deal of detail. What has the poet chosen to describe and why?

■   How has the poet used language to create vivid pictures in the reader's mind?

■   The poem has a dream-like quality. How is this achieved?

■   Although the poem is largely about death and decay, its tone is neither depressing nor negative. What is the tone of the poem and how is it created?

■   Discuss the importance of the last verse, in particular the use of the words 'dead', 'lost grave' and 'sweetness'.

Your discussion of the above points will help you when you come to write an appreciation of this poem.

14   To A Crippled Schoolmaster by Mervyn Morris

a Write a critical appreciation of this poem, focusing in particular on the gradual decline of the schoolmaster's health and the ambivalence of the relationship between teacher and pupil.

b Write a descriptive piece about the final meeting between the schoolmaster and his ex-pupil. Use as many ideas from the poem as is necessary to set the scene and develop the characters.

15   To A Crippled Schoolmaster by Mervyn Morris and The Family by Jenny Fromer

Discuss how the theme of guilt is treated in these poems.

16   The Strangers by Robert Morgan

Write a critical appreciation of this poem. Addressing the following points will help you:

■   Pick out the words and phrases used to describe the old couple, their house, their garden, their world.
Do you notice any pattern emerging in the choice of language? What effect is the poet trying to achieve?

■   What is the poet's attitude towards their world, and indeed, his own?

■   What words and phrases are used to suggest that there is no meeting point between these two worlds? E.g. 'behind hedges', 'locked gate'.

■   Comment on the poet's use of alliteration and assonance, especially in the fourth verse. How does this contribute to the impact of the poem?

■   What is significant about the title of the poem? Who are the 'strangers'?

17   Dick Straightup by Ted Hughes

This poem is particularly dense and vivid in its language and requires careful reading and discussion. The following points are designed to help you think about the poem as a whole and could provide a starting point for your critical appreciation.

■   Identify what each verse is about in terms of the story of the poem.

■   Why does Dick Straightup's presence intimidate the young men? How are we made aware of this?

■   How are we meant to feel about this man? What qualities does Hughes suggest he possesses and how are these conveyed?

■   In what ways is Dick Straightup heroic?

■   Why is his death recorded as some sort of triumph rather than a cause for sadness?

■   Examine the change of tone in the obituary. How would the poem be different without these last six lines?

■   Pick out five words or phrases from the poem which you found particularly striking and say why.

What's it like out there?

We all live in different places and where we live can affect the way we are and what we are able to do with our lives. In these poems, you will read about many different environments – some you might like, others you certainly wouldn't. Read on and make your choice . . .

■ *The Door*

Go and open the door
    Maybe outside there's
    a tree or a wood
    a garden
    or a magic city

Go and open the door
    Maybe a dog's rummaging
Maybe you'll see a face
or an eye
or the picture
                  of a picture

Go and open the door
    If there's a fog
    it will clear . . .

Go and open the door
    Even if there's only
    the darkness ticking,
    even if there's only
    the hollow wind
    even if
            nothing
                is there
go and open the door.

At least
there'll be

a draught.

Miroslav Holub ▓

Going Away and Returning

The best of going away is the going –
That inland sea view
Glimpsed through gaps in a traffic queue;
White mosques on stilts of a pier striding
Towards empty horizons blue with dreaming.

Jolted, we arrive
At Bella Vista gleaming
Gull-grey on a grey parade
Where tired waves at high-tide flap-
Flop, slopping on grey stones.

Later the swept shore is sad
With deck-chair sleepers, paddling children, mad
Mothers grabbing their infants from the sea,
Couples linked by hoarse transistors,
Picnic-papers,
Castles built to be washed away,
And shells,
Scoured, gathered, taken home
To a blind house that smells
Of lack and damp.

Return is dead flowers
In the same vase;
That letter unanswered on the fridge;
Floor unswept;
Clock stopped; range
Cold – the worst of coming back is the kept
Secret of a locked house,
Ourselves on the outside, strange.

Phoebe Hesketh

fasten your seat belts says the voice
inside the plane you can hear no noise
engines made by rolls-royce
take your choice
make mine majorca

check out the parachutes can't be found
alert the passengers they'll be drowned
a friendly mug says settle down
when i come round i'm gagged and bound
for majorca

here comes the neat hostess
and her unapproachable flip finesse
i found the meaning of the word excess
they've got little bags if you want to make a mess
i fancied cuba but it cost a lot less
to majorca
(whose blonde sand fondly kisses the cool fathoms
of the blue mediterranean)

they packed us into the white hotel
you could still smell the polycell
and the white paint in the air-conditioned cells
the waiter smells of fake chanel
gauloises garlic as well
said if i like i could call him miguel
well really

i got drunk with another fella
who'd just brought up a previous paella
wanted a fight but said they were yella
in majorca

the guitars rang the castinets clicked
the dancers stamped the dancers kicked
the double diamond flowed like sick
mother's pride tortilla and chips
pneumatic drills you can't kip
take a dip you're in the shit
if you sing in the street you're knicked
in majorca

the heat made me sick i had to stay in the shade
must have been something in the lemonade
but by the balls of franco i paid
i had to pawn my bucket and spade
next year i take the international brigade
to majorca

John Cooper Clarke

■ *Out in the City*

When you're out in the city
Shuffling down the street,
A bouncy city rhythm
Starts to boogie in your feet.

It jumps off the pavement,
There's a snare drum in your brain,
It pumps through your heart
Like a diesel train.

There's Harry on the corner,
Sings, 'How she goin' boy?'
To loose and easy Winston
With his brother Leroy.

Shout, 'Hello!' to Billy Brisket
With his tripes and cows heels,
Blood-stained rabbits
And trays of live eels.

Maltese Tony
Smoking in the shade
Keeping one good eye
On the amusement arcade.

And everybody's talking:

Move along
Step this way
Here's a bargain
What you say?
Mind your backs
Here's your stop
More fares?
Room on top.

Neon lights and take-aways
Gangs of boys and girls
Football crowds and market stalls
Taxi cabs and noise.

From the city cafes
On the smoky breeze
Smells of Indian cooking
Greek and Cantonese.

Well, some people like suburban life
Some people like the sea
Others like the countryside
But it's the city
Yes it's the city
It's the city life
For me.

Gareth Owen

Newspapers and crisp packets
Drunk men with dirty jackets
Old cars with tyres stripped
Rubbish heaps where junk's been tipped
On the South side of the Thames.

Dirty faces, wearing rags
Used matches and ends of fags
Smoke and dirt from old cars
Smashed bottles and cracked jars
On the South side of the Thames.

Old tunnels full of dirt
Old people watching, feelings hurt
Grey walls full of graffiti
Big kids strong and meaty
On the South side of the Thames.

Broken steet-lamp lights the night
Two youths quarrel and have a fight
Rag and bone men on horses and carts
Smoke in the pubs and the sound of darts
On the South side of the Thames.

Brown leaves, shrivelled flowers in a window box
Old ladies with nylon coats, wishing they were fox
Terraced houses pushing out smoke
Kids drinking water, wishing it was Coke
On the South side of the Thames.

James Smith

■ *Chellow Dean*

Walking where once we courted
Down to Chellow Dean
The muddy track skirts the council estate
Built when houses were people sized
And gardens a necessity.
Across the edge of the golf course
The figures tugging brilliant umbrellas
As if they've strayed from some warm riviera
Onto this windy pennine hill.
I search but cannot spy the witch's house
All millstone grit and rounded turrets.
Down in the woods the reservoirs are hidden
My brother sailed them once, in a cardboard box
We kissed there once, drunk with longing
Today they are empty, drained, disappointing.
Sludge and stray car exhausts.
The banks and stone built sides bare and ugly.
My shoes leak.
I cannot see the grassy field
Where we once loved
The smell of hay, the prickling ground
A million miles away.
But when I squeeze your hand with mine
Knitted gloves and all
And you turn those lovely eyes on me
The present is preferred.

Cath Staincliffe ■

▩ *Syringa*

The syringa's out. That's nice for me:
all along Charing Cross Embankment
the sweet dragging scent reinventing
one of my childhood gardens.
Nice for the drunks and drop-outs too,
if they like it. I'm walking to work:
they'll be here all day under the blossom
with their cider and their British sherry
and their carrier-bags of secrets.
There's been a change in the population:
the ones I had names for – Fat Billy,
the Happy Couple, the Lady with the Dog –
have moved on or been moved off.
But it doesn't do to wonder:
staring hurts in two directions. Once
a tall man chased me here, and I ran
for no good reason: afraid, perhaps,
of turning into Mrs Toothless
with her ankle-socks and her pony-tailed skull
whose eyes avoided mine so many mornings.
And she's gone too. The place has been,
as whatever office will have termed it,
cleaned up. Except that it's not clean
and not really a place: a hesitation
between the traffic fumes and a fragrance,
where this evening I shall walk again.

Fleur Adcock ▩

■ *Darlingford*

Blazing tropical sunshine
On a hard, white dusty road
That curves round and round
Following the craggy coastline;
Coconut trees fringing the coast,
Thousands and thousands
Of beautiful coconut trees,
Their green and brown arms
Reaching out in all directions –
Reaching up to high heaven
And sparkling in the sunshine.
Sea coast, rocky sea coast,
Rocky palm-fringed coastline;
Brown-black rocks,
White sea-foam spraying the rocks;
Waves, sparkling waves
Dancing merrily with the breeze;
The incessant song
Of the mighty sea,
A white sail – far out
Far, far out at sea;
A tiny sailing boat –
White sails all glittering
Flirting with the bright rays
Of the soon setting sun,
Trying to escape their kisses,
In vain – and the jealous winds
Waft her on, on, out to sea
Till sunset; then weary
Of their battle with the sun
The tired winds
Fold themselves to sleep
And the noble craft
No longer idolized
By her two violent lovers
Drifts slowly into port

In the pale moonlight;
Gone are the violent caresses
Of the sun and restless winds –
She nestles in the cool embrace
Of quiet waves
And tender moonlight
Southern silvery moonlight
Shining from a pale heaven
Upon a hard, white, dusty road
That curves round and round
Following the craggy coastline
Of Jamaica's southern shore.

Una Marson

City Johannesburg

This way I salute you:
My hand pulses to my back trousers pocket
Or into my inner jacket pocket
For my pass, my life,
Jo'burg City.
My hand like a starved snake rears my pockets
For my thin, ever lean wallet,
While my stomach groans a friendly smile to hunger,
Jo'burg City.
My stomach also devours coppers and papers
Don't you know?
Jo'burg City, I salute you;
When I run out, or roar in a bus to you,
I leave behind me, my love,
My comic houses and people, my *dongas and my ever whirling
    dust,
My death,

*dongas: steep-sided gulleys created by soil erosion

That's so related to me as a wink to the eye.
Jo'burg City
I travel on your black and white and robotted roads,
Through your thick iron breath that you inhale,
At six in the morning and exhale from five noon.
Jo'burg City
That is the time when I come to you,
When your neon flowers flaunt from your electrical wind,
That is the time when I leave you,
When your neon flowers flaunt their way through the falling
    darkness
On your cement trees.
And as I go back, to my love,
My dongas, my dust, my people, my death,
Where death lurks in the dark like a blade in the flesh,
I can feel your roots, anchoring your might, my feebleness
In my flesh, in my mind, in my blood,
And everything about you says it,
That, that is all you need of me.
Jo'burg City, Johannesburg,
Listen when I tell you,
There is no fun, nothing, in it.
When you leave the women and men with such frozen
    expressions,
Expressions that have tears like furrows of soil erosion,
Jo'burg City, you are like death,
Jo'burg City, Johannesburg, Jo'burg City.

Mongane Wally Serote ▨

110

■ *Touch*

When I get out
I'm going to ask someone
    to touch me
    very gently please
    and slowly,
    touch me
    I want
    to learn again
    how life feels.

I've not been touched
for seven years
    for seven years
    I've been untouched
    out of touch
    and I've learnt
    to know now
    the meaning of
    untouchable.

Untouched – not quite
I can count the things
that have touched me

One: fists
At the beginning
    fierce mad fists
    beating beating
    till I remember
    screaming
    Don't touch me
    please don't touch me.

Two: paws
The first four years of paws
   every day
   patting paws, searching
   — arms up, shoes off
   legs apart —
   prodding paws, systematic
   heavy, indifferent
   probing away
   all privacy.

I don't want fists and paws
I want
   to want to be touched
   again
   and to touch,
   I want to feel alive
   again
   I want to say
   when I get out
Here I am
please touch me.

Hugh Lewin

■ *Freedom*

(Holloway, Spring 1969)

Here at least, I thought,
I shall find freedom.
Here in prison all encumbrances
will be removed.
I shall be left without the burden of
possessions, responsibilities, relationships.
Alone and naked I shall feel
a fresh wind over my entire uncluttered body
blow each pore clear,
cooling and cleaning every crevice.

At last I shall know the relief of
simply obeying orders,
owning nothing,
caring for no one,
being uncared for.

I shall sit content for hours on end
in a bare cell,
glad to be cut off from
things, people, commitments and the
confusing world outside.

But I was wrong.
There is no freedom here –
prison is the world in microcosm.

In my locker is a cache of valuables:
needle, cotton, nail-file, pencil.
My wages buy me fruit and biscuits which
I hoard and hide,
fearing they'll get stolen.

Meticulously I arrange the flowers that
outside friends send in;
carefully decorate my cell with cut out pictures;
get flustered if I lose my mug or bucket.

114

I am no hermit from the outside world,
but strain through busy days to read
each item in the newspapers.
International problems follow me inside;
a prisoner is picked on – she is coloured.

Every evening I am forced to choose
between a range of recreations:
I may read or dance or take a bath,
go to class, play darts or
watch the news.

I am seldom on my own:
a geometry of love, hate, friendship
forms about me.
Someone calls my name,
enters my cell,
asks a favour,
makes some claim upon me.

And I marvel
as I lie alone at night
that this world is as complex as the other;
that even here in jail I am not free to
lose my freedom.

Pat Arrowsmith

■ *On Midsummer Common*

On midsummer common
it's too good to be true
backdrop of cricketers
punts on the river
the champ of horses

and mayflies in June
mere midsummer commonplace.

Not in midsummer,
but with the real rain of more normal weather
putting a different slant on things,
my hard edged steel town
seen through the blur of bus windows.
Saturday afternoon streets crammed
with shoppers under leaden skies.
Out of the constant comedown of the rain, old men
in the final comedown of old age
file into public libraries to turn no pages.
Saturday. My town
can't contain itself.
Roars rise and fall
stadiums spill
football crowds in columns
in the teeming rain.
Saturday buses are jampacked with football rowdies
all going over the score.
I am overlapped by all the fat and laughing losers
that pour from bingo parlours.
Outside cinemas, steadies
queue steadily to buy
their darkness by the square foot.
The palais and troc are choc-full
of gaudy girls dressed parrot fashion.
Saturday's all
social clubs, singers, swilled ale.

So much is spilt —
the steel clang, the clash of creeds,
the overflow of shouts and songs,
the sprawl of litter,
the seep of smells,
the sweat, the vinegar, the beer —
so much slops
into that night nothing goes gentle into,
not even rain.

such a town
I feel at home to be at odds with.

Here on midsummer common
on a midsummer Saturday
you, this day, this place and I
are just exchanging pleasantries.
Oh, it's nice here, but
slagheaps and steelworks
hem my horizons
and something compels
me forge my ironies from a steel town.

Liz Lochhead

Up at Huw's farm nature
Is invading gently, fingering
Its way over a wilderness of deserted
Relics. Here, Huw, Rachel
And two sons once toiled
On a bare hill blotted
With cones of slag and memories.
Now shattered windows grin
Under creeping green locks
And the rude wind mocks
The empty rooms inhabited
By the curious sad silence of
Vanished people and homely residue.
Out in the brambled yard a rust
Crippled plough is sinking into
Forgotten soil and a toppled
Dry wall lets in the tide of
Couch grass from the hill breast.
Down in the valley, pits,
Vague through dust and smoke,
Whisper the dark fugue of
Industry and stubborn faith
Under a chapel eye of God.

Robert Morgan ▨

■ A Small War

Climbing from Merthyr through the dew of August mornings
When I was a centaur-cyclist, on the skills of wheels
I'd loop past the Storey Arms, past streaming lorries
Stopped for flasks of early tea, and fall into Breconshire.
A thin road under black Fan Frynych – which keeps its winter
Shillings long through Spring – took me to the Senni valley.

That was my plenty, to rest on the narrow saddle
Looking down on the farms, letting the simple noises
Come singly up. It was there I saw a ring-ousel
Wearing the white gash of his mountains; but every
Sparrow's feather in that valley was rare, golden,
Perfect. It was an Eden fourteen miles from home.

Evan Drew, my second cousin, lived there, a long, slow man
With a brown gaze I remember him. From a hill farm
Somewhere on the slopes above Heol Senni he sent his sons,
Boys a little older than I, to the second World War.
They rode their ponies to the station, they waved
Goodbye, they circled the spitting sky above Europe.

I would not fight for Wales, the great battle-cries
Do not arouse me. I keep short boundaries holy,
Those my eyes have recognized and my heart has known
As welcome. Nor would I fight for her language. I spend
My few pence of Welsh to amuse my friends, to comment
On the weather. They carry no thought that could be mine.

It's the small wars I understand. So now that forty
People lock their gates in Senni, keeping the water out
With frailest barriers of love and anger, I'd fight for them.
Five miles of land, enough small farms to make a heaven,
Are easily trapped on the drawing-board, a decision
Of the pen drowns all. Yes, the great towns need

The humming water, yes, I have taken my roads to other
Swimming valleys and happily fished above the vanished
Fields. I know the arguments. It is a handful of earth
I will not argue with, and the slow cattle swinging weightily
Home. When I open the taps in my English bathroom
I am surprised they do not run with Breconshire blood.

Leslie Norris ▨

▨ Windscale

The toadstool towers infest the shore:
Stink-horns that propagate and spore
    Wherever the wind blows.
Scafell looks down from the bracken band,
And sees hell in a grain of sand,
    And feels the canker itch between his toes.

This is a land where dirt is clean,
And poison pasture, quick and green,
    And storm sky, bright and bare;
Where sewers flow with milk, and meat
Is carved up for the fire to eat,
    And children suffocate in God's fresh air.

Norman Nicholson ▨

▓ *No More Hiroshimas*

At the station exit, my bundle in hand,
Early the winter afternoon's wet snow
Falls thinly round me, out of a crudded sun.
I had forgotten to remember where I was.
Looking about, I see it might be anywhere –
A station, a town like any other in Japan,
Ramshackle, muddy, noisy, drab; a cheerfully
Shallow permanence: peeling concrete, litter, 'Atomic
Lotion, for hair fall-out,' a flimsy department-store;
Racks and towers of neon, flashy over tiled and tilted waves
Of little roofs, shacks cascading lemons and persimmons,
Oranges and dark-red apples, shanties awash with rainbows
Of squid and octopus, shellfish, slabs of tuna, oysters, ice,
Ablaze with fans of soiled nude-picture books
Thumbed abstractedly by schoolboys, with second-hand looks.

The river remains unchanged, sad, refusing rehabilitation.
In this long, wide, empty official boulevard
The new trees are still small, the office blocks
Basely functional, the bridge a slick abstraction.
But the river remains unchanged, sad, refusing rehabilitation.

In the city centre, far from the station's lively squalor,
A kind of life goes on, in cinemas and hi-fi coffee bars,
In the shuffling racket of pin-table palaces and parlours,
The souvenir-shops piled with junk, kimonoed kewpie-dolls,
Models of the bombed Industry Promotion Hall, memorial ruin
Tricked out with glitter-frost and artificial pearls.

Set in an awful emptiness, the modern tourist hotel is trimmed
With jaded Christmas frippery, flatulent balloons; in the hall,
A giant dingy iced cake in the shape of a Cinderella coach.
The contemporary stairs are treacherous, the corridors
Deserted, my room an overheated morgue, the bar in darkness.
Punctually, the electric chimes ring out across the tidy waste
Their doleful public hymn – the tune unrecognisable, evangelist.

Here atomic peace is geared to meet the tourist trade.
Let it remain like this, for all the world to see,
Without nobility or loveliness, and dogged with shame
That is beyond all hope of indignation. Anger, too, is dead.
And why should memorials of what was far
From pleasant have the grace that helps us to forget?

In the dying afternoon, I wander dying round the Park of Peace.
It is right, this squat, dead place, with its left-over air
Of an abandoned International Trade and Tourist Fair.
The stunted trees are wrapped in straw against the cold.
The gardeners are old, old women in blue bloomers, white aprons,
Survivors weeding the dead brown lawns around the Children's
      Monument.

A hideous pile, the Atomic Bomb Explosion Centre, freezing cold,
'Includes the Peace Tower, a museum containing
Atomic-melted slates and bricks, photos showing
What the Atomic Desert looked like, and other
Relics of the catastrophe.'

The other relics:
The ones that made me weep;
The bits of burnt clothing,
The stopped watches, the torn shirts.
The twisted buttons,
The stained and tattered vests and drawers,
The ripped kimonos and charred boots,
The white blouse polka-dotted with atomic rain, indelible,
The cotton summer pants the blasted boys crawled home in, to bleed
And slowly die.

Remember only these.
They are the memorials we need.

James Kirkup

oral work

Here are some suggestions of activities arising from the poems which involve talking, listening, discussing and even performing. Some of these ideas might lead to written assignments, but that is up to you and your teacher.

performing poems

It is always better to hear a poem than just to read it, but some poems are best when performed. To perform a poem in a group, you need to consider the following points:

■ How many 'parts' could you make? How can the poem be divided up into different voices?

■ Think like a performer. How should people say the lines? Are any actions, sound effects or props needed?

■ You will need to rehearse. Should people learn their lines? Everyone will need a copy of the poem so they know which is their part.

If you take all these points into consideration, your poem should come to life.

The following poems are ideal for performance. You will probably find others which work too. A good size for a group is four people. After the performance, get into groups to discuss how it went. Ideas are provided for further discussion on each poem.

Whichever poem your group chooses to perform, you will introduce it with a reading of **'The Door' by Miroslav Holub**. This short poem provides an ideal introduction to thinking about different places.

Here are some suggestions to help you perform 'The Door':

1 Will one person read it, or will the group divide it up? If so, how?

2 Think carefully about the mood of the poem. Does it change and if so, where?

3 This poem probably works best if you change the volume of your voice as you perform it. Are there certain lines or verses which should be spoken softly?

4 Think carefully about the last three lines. What mood and volume are best here?

5 Do you want to include any actions?

▓ *Majorca*   *by John Cooper Clarke*

Before you discuss this poem, you should have prepared 'The Door'.

To start

Each person in the group reads the poem to themselves, then listens to one member of the group reading it out loud. Now work through these points:

1 Look up any unfamiliar vocabulary.

2 There is no punctuation in this poem, so you must work out exactly where the pauses come.

3 There are two pronunciations of the name 'Majorca'. Find out what they are and decide which one is more suitable for the poem.

4 Decide how you will divide up the poem for performance. Taking it verse by verse is not the only way. Experiment with alternating lines and splitting verses. Are there any lines you want to say altogether as a group?

5 How will you say the two lines in brackets?

6 Although the tone of the poem stays the same, there are certain words and phrases which need to be emphasised. Discuss which these may be and how you will perform them.

7 Are there any actions which could help your performance and bring out the humour of the poem?

When you have had your discussions and made your decisions, you are ready to start rehearsing.

After the performance

This holiday to Majorca certainly didn't live up to the promises in the brochure. Why do people go on holidays like this? In your group, discuss any holiday experiences you have had and whether the whole idea of 'going on holiday' is a good one. Why do people feel such a need to have a change of surroundings every year?

Out in the City   *by Gareth Owen*

Before you discuss this poem, you should have prepared 'The Door'.

To start

Each person in the group reads the poem to themselves, then listens to one member of the group reading it out loud. Now work through these points:

1 Decide how you are going to divide this poem. Will you divide it into characters? Will you use a narrator? Think about this carefully.

2 How will you perform the verse written in italics?

3 Are there any lines which the group could say together?

4 How will the last four lines be performed?

5 Are there any actions you could use which would help you bring out the meaning of this poem?

When you have had your discussions and made your decisions, you are ready to start rehearsing.

After the performance

Gareth Owen has selected details which show what he enjoys about life in the city. What do you like about the place where you live? What details would you pick out which best sum up your thoughts and feelings about the place?

Before you discuss this poem, you should have prepared 'The Door'.

To start

Each person in the group reads the poem to themselves, then listens to one member of the group reading it out loud. Now work through these points:

1   Where do you think this person is?

2   Is it possible to divide the poem into those lines spoken directly by the character, and those which could be performed by other members of the group? Can the poem be divided in terms of past, present and future? Think about these things carefully.

3   The poem has very distinct mood changes. What are they? Where do they occur and how will you reflect these in your performance?

4   Are there any words or lines which could be spoken by the group together?

5   Can you think of any actions or movements which would add to the impact of your performance?

6   The word 'touch' is repeated many times, by itself or as part of a word. Look at each example and experiment with different ways of saying it. Here are some suggestions: angrily, pleadingly, softly, defiantly, pathetically, optimistically.

7   Think carefully about the pace and volume of your performance. How can both of these be used to greatest effect?

When you have had your discussions and made your decisions, you are ready to start rehearsing.

After the performance

When we think about our senses, it is usually sight and hearing we most fear losing. In his poem, Hugh Lewin writes about touch in a surprising way. In your groups, discuss the relative value of all five senses and their importance in our everyday lives.

■ *On Midsummer Common*   *by Liz Lochhead*

Before you discuss this poem, you should have prepared 'The Door'.

To start

Each person in the group reads the poem to themselves, then listens to one member of the group reading it out loud. Now work through these points:

1   You will need to study carefully the sentence structure and the placing of full stops in order to bring out the full meaning of the poem.

2   How will you divide the poem? There are several choices – experiment and see which way works best.

3   How will you bring out the contrast between the first and last verses and the rest of the poem in terms of tone, volume and pace? Should the same person start and end the performance?

4   The poet uses alliteration and assonance to create some of her effects. Find out what these terms mean and identify where they are used in the poem. Make sure your performance is sensitive to the use of these techniques.

When you have had your discussions and made your decisions, you are ready to start rehearsing.

After the performance

In the poem, Liz Lochhead focuses on people as members of crowds. In your group, discuss your experiences of being part of a large crowd. You should think about the feelings it arouses, for example, fear, exhilaration, and try to say why it is that people behave differently when they are part of a large gathering. Also think of the sorts of occasions when people are crowded together – pop concerts, football matches, cinema/theatres, school, political rallies or demonstrations, sporting events. How does behaviour differ in these circumstances?

other suggestions for oral work

1 Give a talk to the class lasting five to ten minutes on one of the following:

- The area where I live.
- My favourite place.
- My ideal/dream place.

2 Best place/worst place

a Working in pairs, look carefully through this section and discuss which poems, in your opinion, describe the worst place and best place to be. Give clear reasons for your choice when you report back to the class.

b From personal experience discuss the places you've lived in or visited which fall into the above categories. Prepare a short talk on this for the class. (A place does not necessarily have to be a large area, it could be somewhere as small as your bedroom.)

3 Every picture tells a story

Your task in this assignment is to discuss in groups which six environments (places) you would choose to photograph if you were putting together a display entitled 'Britain Today'. You must think of Britain as a whole, not just your area, so that if you were to show the six photographs to someone from another country, they would have a clear picture of the variety of environments in Britain. In your discussion, you must describe exactly what you would photograph and be able to justify your choice to the rest of the class when you report back.

4 Working by yourself or in pairs, choose your favourite poem from this section. How could you present it to the rest of the class? Your task is to give a ten-minute lesson using the poem either by itself or with other materials, in a way which will keep the class interested and involved.

5 One of the most effective ways to convey the atmosphere of a place is to appeal to the reader's senses. The poets in this section have used this technique particularly well, not only describing what they see and hear but also what they can touch, taste and smell.

a In your groups, work through the poems, recording in five columns the sense images you find most powerful.

b Look closely at all the sense images you have collected and decide as a group which five you like best and why.

c Report your findings to the rest of the class. Is it possible for the class as a whole to agree on a final five?

6   Connections

a As a class, identify the obvious places you all have in common – for example, the same school, same town/area etc.

b In pairs (with someone you don't usually work with), you have two minutes to talk and discover a place in common. It could be somewhere you've visited, have relations, or perhaps have been to for entertainment. Each pair should then report back to the class.

c Now, in fours, repeat the above exercise. This time you have four minutes. Report back.

Is it possible to find one place the whole class has in common and never realised before?

written work

The written work has been divided into two sections: Language assignments and Literature assignments. Within each section, there are opportunities to write in a variety of ways about the poems you have read. The range of written work is designed to meet the requirements of whichever GCSE examination course you are doing. Your teacher will help you to select the right assignments for you and your course.

language assignments

1 The following lines are taken from poems in this section. Choose one of them and use it as the first line of a story:

■ When I get out ...

■ There is no freedom here.

■ It's too good to be true.

■ Saturday – my town.

■ I had forgotten to remember where I was.

■ I am seldom on my own.

2 Write two contrasting descriptions of places. They can be places you know, or from your imagination. Each description must cover at least a side and a half of A4 paper. Here are some suggestions:

■ The same place at different times of the day or different seasons.

■ A busy place and a quiet place.

■ An urban setting and a rural setting.

■ A landscape and a seascape.

Do not simply describe what these places look like, think about all five senses and spend some time selecting vocabulary and images which will create the appropriate atmosphere.

3 Wish you were here ...

The job of a travel brochure writer is to sell holidays. In order to do this, they must make places sound as attractive as possible and point out all the advantages of going there.

a Your first task in this assignment is to produce a mini brochure on a place of your choice. This could be your own area, somewhere you've already visited or an imaginary tropical island. To help you start, look at a range of travel brochures to give you some ideas on layout and style of writing. You must produce:

- A map of the area.

- General information about travel, climate, history etc.

- Details of accommodation.

- Details of local facilities.

- Details of places of interest to visit; local customs; annual events.

- Prices.

You may include pictures if you wish.

b Imagine you are a traveller who has just returned from the holiday advertised in the brochure. You were not satisfied and felt that the brochure deliberately misled you. Write a letter of complaint to the travel company outlining the reasons for your dissatisfaction.

4

Choose a title from one of the poems in this section and use it as a starting point for a story.

5

This assignment gives you the opportunity to say what you think about some of the issues raised by the poems in this section.

a Wherever you live, you will be aware of the kind of pressures associated with living in a big city. Newspapers and television documentaries seem to focus on inner city problems, but those living outside the city will know pressures exist there too. We hear less and less about the pleasures to be gained from both urban and rural life.

Write an essay exploring the pressures and pleasures of these two contrasting environments.

b There are several poems in this section which make it clear that our environment isn't just what we see out of our windows. Our lives are shaped by the decisions of those in power and every country has its own identifiable 'political environment'. Nowhere is this made more clear than in the poem 'City Johannesburg' by Mongane Wally Serote, which is as much about the political system of apartheid as the city itself.

Choose three different political environments from around the world and show how they affect the lives of the people in those countries. If you wish, you can focus on particular groups in society and how they fare under different regimes.

c Nuclear energy – a curse or a blessing?

d Prisons do not reform – they merely punish. Discuss.

e Saving the environment is the greatest challenge humanity has to face in the twenty-first century. Discuss.

f Throughout history, individuals, families or whole communities have up-rooted and moved to new areas or even countries. Explore the reasons behind this movement of people to new environments.

6 Personal writing

Choose one of the following:

a Write about three places which have been important to you at different stages in your life. They could be places you've lived or visited, or associate with particular people. Describe each place in detail and say why it holds special significance to you. For the purpose of this assignment, the place can be anything from a room to a country.

b Best place/worst place – describe two places from your experience which fall into these categories. Write at least a side and a half of A4 paper on each.

7 Write a play about a family arguing over where to go on holiday. Each member of the family has different ideas about what they want and tries to persuade the others to their point of view. Show how the argument develops and how it is finally resolved. You can base this on your own family if you wish or an entirely imaginary one. You should have a maximum of five characters.

8 Imagine those responsible for either the dropping of the atom bomb on Hiroshima or the building of the Windscale Power Station are put on trial. Write a transcript of the trial, imagining yourself in the role of the barrister either defending or prosecuting these people. Though the poems 'Windscale' or 'No More Hiroshimas' could provide a starting point, some research will be necessary in order for you to bring out important information and evidence to build up your case. The 'trial' should be written in play form.

literature assignments

1 The title of this section asks 'What's it Like Out There?' Which two poets, in your opinion, have given the most effective answer?

2 The poems in this section describe a great variety of places. In this assignment, write about four poems – two which describe places you would like to visit, and two describing places you would hate. You should make the reasons for your choices clear by referring closely to the details in each poem.

3 Choose two poems from this section – one you liked and one you didn't. Write a letter to each of the poets, explaining in detail the reasons for your response. Justify your comments by referring closely to each of the poems. Each letter should cover at least a side and a half of A4 paper.

4 Choose three to five poems from this section and say why you liked them.

5 Select one of the following:

a *Down Your Way* is a weekly programme on Radio 4, where listeners are asked to give a short talk on what life is like where they live. Choose three poems from this section which describe different places, and imagine what a person who lived in each of them would have to say if they were presenting a talk on *Down Your Way*. Although you will have to refer closely to the details in the poems, avoid copying whole lines or sections. Concentrate instead on how the person feels about the place in which they live. You should aim to cover at least a side of A4 paper for each talk.

b Using as many poems as you can from this section, demonstrate how an environment has the power to shape the lives of those who live within it and make them behave the way they do.

c Using as many poems as you can from this section, demonstrate how people have the power to shape the environment in which they live, usually with detrimental effects.

6 Compare and contrast the different views of city life depicted in this section.

7 Majorca by John Cooper Clarke and Darlingford by Una Marson

a 'Majorca' is intended to be humorous. Pick out six examples of lines or sections where the poet succeeded in making you laugh and explain how he achieved this effect.

b When we go on holiday, we expect to enjoy ourselves. The character in 'Majorca' obviously didn't. If, however, you had visited the southern shore of Jamaica, as described in the poem 'Darlingford', you would have had a very different experience. Write two letters to a travel company. In the first letter, imagine you are the man who went to Majorca and complain about how unsatisfactory the holiday was. In the second letter, imagine you have visited Darlingford and thank the travel company for recommending such a beautiful place.

8 Going Away and Returning by Phoebe Hesketh and Majorca by John Cooper Clarke

a 'Majorca' is intended to make us laugh. It presents a stereotypical view of package holidays in which the holiday makers are as much at fault as the resort itself. With close reference to diction, rhyming pattern, imagery and use of contrast in the poem, show how the humour is achieved.

b Show how both poems, in their different ways, demonstrate the futility of holidays.

9 Out in the City by Gareth Owen and South Side by James Smith

Gareth Owen is an established poet whereas James Smith wrote his poem as a piece of English homework. If Gareth Owen had visited James Smith in school, what might they have said to each other about their reasons for writing their city poems? Write a conversation in play form between the two poets, bringing out their different feelings about city life and why they each selected the images they did. If you wish, add other characters to the play who could provide extra comments and questions on the two poems. They might be James Smith's English teacher and some of the pupils in his class.

10 On Midsummer Common by Liz Lochhead, Chellow Dean by Cath Staincliffe and Syringa by Fleur Adcock

All three poems are about memories associated with place. Explore what effect each poet hoped to achieve and how successful they were. Complete your assignment with a paragraph stating which of the three poems you preferred and why.

11 Darlingford by Una Marson and City Johannesburg by Mongane Wally Serote

In 'Darlingford', Una Marson describes an idyllic setting in Jamaica, while Mongane Wally Serote effectively evokes the living hell of Johannesburg. Show how each poet has successfully managed to communicate the power of place.

12 Darlingford by Una Marson

a Una Marson has made Darlingford seem like most people's idea of Paradise. Which words and phrases has she used to create this impression? Make a list. Pick out the five you liked best and for each one describe why you think it is effective and what sort of picture it conjured up in your mind.

b Using the ideas from **a** write a paragraph for a holiday brochure describing Darlingford. Look at some brochures first to give you some help with the language, style and layout you will need to use. You can add a picture, if you wish.

c The middle section of the poem is about the effects of the sun and the wind on the 'tiny sailing boat'. Una Marson calls the sun and wind 'Two violent lovers'. Say why you think this is a good description and pick out all the other words and phrases which are connected with this idea, for example, 'flirting'. Why do you think she chose to use this particular image in the poem?

13 Touch by Hugh Lewin and Freedom by Pat Arrowsmith

Show how, in their different ways, these two poems make powerful statements about imprisonment and the contrasting effects it has on the two individuals portrayed.

14   On Midsummer Common by Liz Lochhead

With close reference to language and imagery, show how Liz Lochhead builds up a picture of her home town as a place she feels 'at home to be at odds with'. How is this feeling heightened by her Saturday on Midsummer Common?

15   A Small War by Leslie Norris

Write a critical appreciation of this poem. Addressing the following points will help you:

■ What do the following phrases convey to you: 'centaur cyclist'; 'that was my plenty'; 'Eden'; 'frailest barriers of love and anger' and 'a decision of the pen drowns all'?

■ What makes the Senni Valley so special to the character in the poem? Comment on the use of detail.

■ 'It's the small wars I understand'. What does the poet mean by this and how is this belief demonstrated in the poem?

■ 'I know the arguments'. What are they? What contradictions do they hold?

■ Explain the last two lines of the poem.

■ What is the tone of this poem and how does it change?

■ This poem was written in support of a cause. Does it succeed in persuading the reader that flooding the Senni Valley would be a tragedy?

16   No More Hiroshimas by James Kirkup

For a full understanding of this poem, you should acquaint yourself with the facts about the atomic explosion in Hiroshima in August 1945.

■ Look up any unfamiliar vocabulary.

■ Each verse represents a different view of present-day Hiroshima. Look at each one and identify what aspect of the city it describes. Does any pattern emerge? Is there a change of tone?

■ In the first verse, Kirkup describes the normality of Hiroshima – 'it might be anywhere'. How is this an effective opening to the poem?

■ How do the details in verses 2, 3 and 4 prepare us for the sentiments expressed in verse 5? How would you describe the tone of this verse? In what sense is it a climax to the poem?

- What clues are there in the poem that the catastrophic effects of the explosion still have repercussions for the citizens of Hiroshima and their environment? Why does Kirkup use the phrase 'A kind of life goes on'?

- The visit to Hiroshima takes place at Christmas. What does this add to the poem?

- In the penultimate verse, the style changes. Why do you suppose Kirkup chose to do this? What is significant about the images he has chosen in this verse and what effect do they have on the reader?

- What do the last two lines of the poem mean? Why did Kirkup choose to end it in this way?

- What is the significance of the title?

- 'No More Hiroshimas' is a very powerful poem. What precisely gives it its power?

Addressing these points will help you to write a critical appreciation of this poem.

Nine to five

'What are you going to do when you leave school?' How many times have you been asked that question? It's a worry deciding what to do with the rest of your life and the choice often seems confusing. These poems not only explore a range of different jobs, but also remind us that you don't necessarily have to earn a wage to be doing a full-time job. What will *you* be doing 'nine to five'?

The Production Line

Nick paints the outside
Stan paints the inside
They do it all through the day
Tom does the nuts up
Bill does the bolts up
They always do it that way
Alf puts the wheels on
Bert puts the tyres on
They fix 'em so they're O.K.
Ted puts the engine
Arthur puts the boot in
But Fred's ill and he's not here today
Len puts the front seat in
George puts the back seat in
They fix 'em so they'll stay
Dan puts the lights on
Henry puts the bumpers on
Waiting for a tea break so they can get away
John puts the steering wheels in
Charlie puts the key in
And drives the car away
They can't stop long
Because as soon as that one's gone
There's another one on the way.

Bobby Pearce ▦

Feminine Advice (Rap)

Like every other mother, mine
was keen to tell her daughter
to certainly go swimming, but
to not go near the water.
To find myself a Good Career
to Travel and Have Fun
and not to tie myself down at eighteen with husband, home
and bloody ungrateful children
like she'd done.
If I cut according to my cloth and didn't
get excited
at around thirty I would find myself miraculously
Mister-Righted.
She said to watch my handbag and keep myself nice.

Oh I sure was grateful for the feminine advice.

But I had a lot to learn when I went to school –
like how women weren't
mechanically minded as a rule.
Headmaster, careers mistress, in subtle alliance
to remind us we were rotten at Maths and Science.
Oh, I really shocked her
when I told her, 'Miss,
I want to be a doctor' –
She asked me had I thought it out? A woman could do worse
than be a nurse.
And 'in fact, with dedication, any bright girl can
be the driving force behind a really Top Man
(and once you've got him, here's how to please –
via his stomach and macaroni surprise)
oh, he'll put you on a pedestal,
he'll treat you like a queen
if you just put your trust
in Pristine Clean –
remember in Office Practice the thing that is most shocking
is turning up with black-rim nails, or splashes in your stocking.

142

So, when you go for interview,
Knees together in navyblue,
Wear little white collars and be quiet as mice . . .'

Oh I sure was grateful for the feminine advice.

And those Women's Mags were always telling you
about thrush, the hot flush and what to do
and how to keep your husband true
and what to dip in your fondue.
How to address Royalty (with the minimum of slanging)
How to unravel old potscourers and torn tights and
Knit them up into an Attractive Wallhanging.
How New Ways With Eyeshadow turn a housewife to a teaser.
How to tan, bake a flan, and plan for your freezer.
How to rescue junkshop finds and strip them for Good Use.
And, especially for Christmas,
Sauce for the goose.
Oh, their serving suggestions sounded awfully nice,

So I sure was grateful for the feminine advice.

Liz Lochhead

From: Six Poems for Hospital Workers

This is a poem for
the hospital orderly
who does the waterjugs
serves the breakfast
serves the tea
gives out the menus
serves the coffee
cleans the lockers
collects the menus
serves the lunch
serves the tea
serves some more tea
and clocks off
Next morning she starts the whole thing again –
does the water jugs
serves the breakfast . . .
This poem is boring.
It gets boring, after eleven years, she says.

This is not a woolworths waitress
(or is it)
This is a nurse in
the new national uniform
Little boy blue gingham and
a paper hat.
She gets electric shocks making the
new king fund beds.
Changing babies nappies would be better
she thinks, stowing disposable bed pans
at least they don't shit so much
all at once

Cleaning under this bed is
the married woman sociology student
who is working all through her vacations
as she doesn't get a grant
(her husband works all through his vacations
as a porter
and gets 30% more)
She has noticed with excitement
how nobody looks at cleaning women
or respects them
Nobody looks at students pretending
to be cleaning women either
(they don't join unions)
Everyone notices her accent
She talks loudly because her husband never listens
'Aren't you rather educated to be a cleaner, cleaner?'
they ask her constantly.
'Oh, you're a student.'
She's going to put it all in her dissertation.
She can't imagine how people who
work there always
put up with it
She gave in her notice today, gratefully
after ten weeks

Here is a poem for
the women who don't write poems
who do the work because work is
and do more work because work is
who are: fast, kind, vacant, fat
service and produce, produce and service
There are no words to write this poem because
they have no words.
Who would do their jobs
if they had words. No more words. The poems over.

Diana Scott

■ *Weekend Glory*

Some dichty folks
don't know the facts,
posin' and preenin'
and puttin' on acts,
stretchin' their necks
and strainin' their backs.

They move into condos
up over the ranks,
pawn their souls
to the local banks.
Buying big cars
they can't afford,
ridin' around town
actin' bored.

If they want to learn how to live life right,
they ought to study me on Saturday night.

My job at the plant
ain't the biggest bet,
but I pay my bills
and stay out of debt.

I get my hair done
for my own self's sake,
so I don't have to pick
and I don't have to rake.

Take the church money out
and head cross town
to my friend girl's house
where we plan our round.
We meet our men and go to a joint
where the music is blues
and to the point.

Folks write about me.
They just can't see
how I work all week
at the factory.
Then get spruced up
and laugh and dance
And turn away from worry
with sassy glance.

They accuse me of livin'
from day to day,
but who are they kiddin'?
So are they.

Maya Angelou ▦

▦ *Labour Exchange*

These men clutching cards, stand in slack groups
Round the stove in the wooden room, fog
Shoving its nose around the door.

The clock keeps a prim eye on them, intent
On supervision, and white with disapproval of
Their profane disillusion and their thick mirth.

They have had a slice of bread and lard;
Warmed their hands at a cup of tea;
Left wives scrubbing in aprons of sacking,

For this, the terminus of hopes and sorrows,
Where the blazing stadium and the satisfaction of food,
Or the cipher of want, daily arrive and depart.

They stand for many hours, obscure,
Glimpsing through windows the autumn sun on
The spires of the world they built, but do not share.

Clifford Dyment ▦

■ 'Maintenance Engineer'

One Friday night it happened, soon after we were wed,
When my old man came in from work as usual I said:
'Your tea is on the table, clean clothes are on the rack,
Your bath will soon be ready, I'll come up and scrub your
   back.'
He kissed me very tenderly and said, 'I'll tell you flat
The service I give my machine ain't half as good as that.'

I said . . .
Chorus
I'm not your little woman, your sweetheart or your dear
I'm a wage slave without wages, I'm a maintenance engineer.

Well then we got to talking. I told him how I felt,
How I keep him running just as smooth as some conveyor
   belt!
Well after all, it's I'm the one provides the power supply
He goes just like the clappers on me steak'n kidney pie.
His fittings are all shining 'cos I keep 'em nice and clean
And he tells me his machine tool is the best I've ever seen.

But . . .
Chorus

The terms of my employment would make your hair turn
   grey,
I have to be on call you see for 24 hours a day.
I quite enjoy the perks though while I'm working through the
   night
For we get job satisfaction. Well he does, and then I might.
If I keep up full production, I should have a kid or two,
So some future boss will have a brand new labour force to
   screw.

So . . .
Chorus

The truth began to dawn then, how I keep him fit and trim
So the boss can make a nice fat profit out of me and him.
And, as a solid union man, he got in quite a rage
To think that we're both working hard and getting one man's
   wage.
I said 'And what about the part-time packing job I do?
That's three men that I work for love, my boss, your boss and
   you.'

So . . .
Chorus

He looked a little sheepish and he said, 'As from today
The lads and me will see what we can do on equal pay.
Would you like a housewives' union? Do you think you
   should get paid?
As a cook and as a cleaner, as a nurse and as a maid?'
I said, 'Don't jump the gun love, if you did your share at
   home,
Perhaps I'd have some time to fight some battles of my own.'

For . . .
Chorus

I've often heard you tell me how you'll pull the bosses down.
You'll never do it brother while you're bossing me around.
'Til women join the struggle, married, single, white and black
You're fighting with a blindfold and one arm behind your
   back.'
The message has got over now for he's realised at last
That power to the sisters must mean power to the class.

And . . .
Chorus
Repeat: I'm not your little woman, your sweetheart or your dear
        I'm a wage-slave without wages
        I'm a maintenance engineer.

Sandra Kerr ▨

The Wife's Tale

When I had spread it all on linen cloth
Under the hedge, I called them over.
The hum and gulp of the thresher ran down
And the big belt slewed to a standstill, straw
Hanging undelivered in the jaws.
There was such quiet that I heard their boots
Crunching the stubble twenty yards away.

He lay down and said 'Give these fellows theirs.
I'm in no hurry,' plucking grass in handfuls
And tossing it in the air. 'That looks well.'
(He nodded at my white cloth on the grass.)
'I declare a woman could lay out a field
Though boys like us have little call for cloths.'
He winked, then watched me as I poured a cup
And buttered the thick slices that he likes.
'It's threshing better than I thought, and mind
It's good clean seed. Away over there and look.'
Always this inspection has to be made
Even when I don't know what to look for.

But I ran my hand in the half-filled bags
Hooked to the slots. It was hard as shot,
Innumerable and cool. The bags gaped
Where the chutes ran back to the stilled drum
And forks were stuck at angles in the ground
As javelins might mark lost battlefields.
I moved between them back across the stubble.

They lay in the ring of their own crusts and dregs
Smoking and saying nothing. 'There's good yield,
Isn't there?' – as proud as if he were the land itself –
'Enough for crushing and for sowing both.'
And that was it. I'd come and he had shown me
So I belonged no further to the work.
I gathered cups and folded up the cloth
And went. But they still kept their ease
Spread out, unbuttoned, grateful, under the trees.

Seamus Heaney

Elegy for Alfred Hubbard

Hubbard is dead, the old plumber;
who will mend our burst pipes now,
the tap that has dripped all the summer,
testing the sink's overflow?

No other like him. Young men with knowledge
of new techniques, theories from books,
may better his work straight from college,
but who will challenge his squint-eyed looks

in kitchen, bathroom, under floorboards,
rules of thumb which were often wrong;
seek as erringly stopcocks in cupboards,
or make a job last half as long?

He was a man who knew the ginnels,
alleyways, streets – the whole district,
family secrets, minor annals,
time-honoured fictions fused to fact.

Seventy years of gossip muttered
under his cap, his tufty thatch,
so that his talk was slow and clotted,
hard to follow, and too much.

As though nothing fell, none vanished,
and time were the maze of Cheetham Hill,
in which the dead – with jobs unfinished –
waited to hear him ring the bell.

For much he never got round to doing,
but meant to, when weather bucked up,
or worsened, or when his pipe was drawing,
or when he'd finished this cup.

I thought time, he forgot so often,
had forgotten him, but here's Death's pomp
over his house, and by the coffin
the son who will inherit his blowlamp,

tools, workshop, cart, and cornet
(pride of Cheetham Prize Brass Band),
and there's his mourning widow, Janet,
stood at the gate he'd promised to mend.

Soon he will make his final journey;
shaved and silent, strangely trim,
with never a pause to talk to any-
body: how arrow-like, for him!

In St Mark's Church, whose dismal tower
he pointed and painted when a lad,
they will sing his praises amidst flowers
while, somewhere, a cellar starts to flood,

and the housewife banging his front-door knocker
is not surprised to find him gone,
and runs for Thwaite, who's a better worker,
and sticks at a job until it's done.

Tony Connor

Woman Enough

Because my grandmother's hours
were apple cakes baking,
& dust motes gathering,
& linens yellowing
& seams and hems
inevitably unravelling –
I almost never keep house –
though really I *like* houses
& wish I had a clean one.

Because my mother's minutes
were sucked into the roar
of the vacuum cleaner,
because she waltzed with the washer-dryer
& tore her hair waiting for repairmen –
I send out my laundry,
& live in a dusty house,
though really I *like* clean houses
as well as anyone.

I am woman enough
to love the kneading of bread
as much as the feel
of typewriter keys
under my fingers –
springy, springy.
& the smell of clean laundry
& simmering soup
are almost as dear to me
as the smell of paper and ink.

I wish there were not a choice;
I wish I could be two women.
I wish the days could be longer.
But they are short.

So I write while
the dust piles up.

I sit at my typewriter
remembering my grandmother
& all my mothers,
& the minutes they lost
loving houses better than themselves –
& the man I love cleans up the kitchen
grumbling only a little
because he knows
that after all these centuries
it is easier for him
than for me.

Erica Jong

Thatcher

Bespoke for weeks, he turned up some morning
Unexpectedly, his bicycle slung
With a light ladder and a bag of knives.
He eyed the old rigging, poked at the eaves,

Opened and handled sheaves of lashed wheat-straw.
Next, the bundled rods: hazel and willow
Were flicked for weight, twisted in case they'd snap.
It seemed he spent the morning warming up:

Then fixed the ladder, laid out well honed blades
And snipped at straw and sharpened ends of rods
That, bent in two, made a white-pronged staple
For pinning down his world, handful by handful.

Couchant for days on sods above the rafters
He shaved and flushed the butts, stitched all together
Into a sloped honeycomb, a stubble patch,
And left them gaping at his Midas touch.

Seamus Heaney

From: Six Men Monologues
No. 5: Mo

Men says My Boss
are definitely more dependable
and though even in these days of equal pay
men tend to come a wee bitty more expensive
due to the added responsibility a man tends to have
in his jobspecification
Well for instance you can depend on a man not to get
pregnant.
My Boss says men are more objective.
Catch a man bitching
about healthhazards and conditions
and going out on strike over no papertowels in the toilet
or nagging over the lack of day nursery facilities
My Boss says as far as he's concerned a crêche is a motor
    accident in Kelvinside
and any self respecting woman should have a good man
to take care of her so it's only pinmoney anyway
and that's bound to come out in the attitude.
Well a man isn't subject to moods
or premenstrual tension a guy
isn't going to phone in sick with some crap about cramps.
My Boss says a man rings in
with an upset stomach and you know either
he means a hangover or else his brother
managed to get him a ticket for Wembley.

You know where you are with a man.

Liz Lochhead ▧

EXECUTIVE

I am a young executive. No cuffs than mine are cleaner;
I have a Slimline brief-case and I use the firm's Cortina.
In every roadside hostelry from here to Burgess Hill
The *maîtres d'hôtel* all know me well and let me sign the bill.

You ask me what it is I do. Well actually, you know,
I'm partly a liaison man and partly P. R. O.
Essentially I integrate the current export drive
And basically I'm viable from ten o'clock till five.

For vital off-the-record work – that's talking transport wise –
I've a scarlet Aston-Martin – and does she go? She flies!
Pedestrians and dogs and cats – we mark them down for slaughter.
I also own a speed-boat which has never touched the water.

She's built of fibre-glass, of course. I call her 'Mandy Jane'
After a bird I used to know – No soda, please, just plain –
And how did I acquire her? Well to tell you about that
And to put you in the picture I must wear my other hat.

I do some mild developing. The sort of place I need
Is a quiet country market town that's rather run to seed.
A luncheon and a drink or two, a little *savoir faire* –
I fix the Planning Officer, the Town Clerk and the Mayor.

And if some preservationist attempts to interfere
A 'dangerous structure' notice from the Borough Engineer
Will settle any buildings that are standing in our way –
The modern style, sir, with respect, has really come to stay.

John Betjeman

Song of the Wagondriver

My first love was the ten-ton truck
They gave me when I started,
And though she played the bitch with me
I grieved when we were parted.

Since then I've had a dozen more,
The wound was quick to heal,
And now it's easier to say
I'm married to my wheel.

I've trunked it north, I've trunked it south,
On wagons good and bad,
But none was ever really like
The first I ever had.

The life is hard, the hours are long,
Sometimes I cease to feel,
But I go on, for it seems to me
I'm married to my wheel.

Often I think of my home and kids,
Out on the road at night,
And think of taking a local job
Provided the money's right.

Two nights a week I see my wife,
And eat a decent meal,
But otherwise, for all my life,
I'm married to my wheel.

B. S. Johnson

Cleator Moor

From one shaft at Cleator Moor
They mined for coal and iron ore.
This harvest below ground could show
Black and red currants on one tree.

In furnaces they burnt the coal,
The ore was smelted into steel,
And railway lines from end to end
Corseted the bulging land.

Pylons sprouted on the fells,
Stakes were driven in like nails;
And the ploughed fields of Devonshire
Were sliced with the steel of Cleator Moor.

The land waxed fat and greedy too,
It would not share the fruits it grew,
And coal and ore, as sloe and plum,
Lay black and red for jamming time.

The pylons rusted on the fells,
The gutters leaked beside the walls,
And women searched the ebb-tide tracks
For knobs of coal or broken sticks.

But now the pits are wick with men,
Digging like dogs dig for a bone:
For food and life *we* dig the earth –
In Cleator Moor they dig for death.

Every wagon of cold coal
Is fire to drive a turbine wheel;
Every knuckle of soft ore
A bullet in a soldier's ear.

The miner at the rockface stands,
With his segged and bleeding hands
Heaps on his head the fiery coal,
And feels the iron in his soul.

Norman Nicholson

■ *Vital*

I think my work is important, I am a link
In a long chain.
I had to have the training for it,
And I had to dirty my hands.
They ask my advice when they want to know
   what would be best.
I might move up even higher, in time.

On Sunday, I woke up shouting. She said,
What on earth's the matter, we're supposed to be
Going out to dinner later; or rather lunch.
I dressed, and played with Lynda, and
Felt a bit better.

I was called into the office from the shop
Floor. 'Mr Fletton, up from London, wants to see you.'
But I was hearing the mutter-mutter,
The kind-of giggling noises inside the machines
Through four thick concrete walls.
I could not read the words in front of my eyes.

She said last Thursday, you haven't said a thing
The whole evening.
I said no. I've been watching:
. . . I couldn't name a thing I'd seen on the screen.

Today is vital, people are relying on me
To get ten thousand packages out on time.
I am part of a chain, a link, they ask my advice.
I open the front door. After the wind,
It's a lovely cool morning, and sun;
Very bright.
The keys of the Toledo are clenched wet
In my right hand. And I don't move.
I am standing shaking. I am standing, shaking.

Alan Brownjohn ■

Book of Stones

For ten decades this river has crawled
In black with pit-poison and blood
On a scarred landscape under a Welsh sky.
There are no sheep on the dead hills of
Sharp slag lifted by distorted hands
From dark places deep in broken earth.
Industrial Readymades darken the sky
And pit-ponds green and calm
Lap beaches of desolate ash,
Wry trees break with brittle cries
In the dust-wind over tombstones of men.
These men, buried with silica scars,
Lie hidden with the same cold rock
Marked long ago by their warm hands.
Their plain history in the Book of Stones,
Now eroded by the wind's work, is unknown
Or forgotten.
                    Where is their memorial?
They gathered the brute harvest deep
In the vaults of earth and made men rich.

Robert Morgan

This poem is printed out of sequence. Please see Literature assignment 16.

Elegy on a Tyneside Shipyard

1 Those days are gone forever.
They'll never come again
But they left their mark behind them
On a thousand broken men.
Now the ships are getting bigger
The tanks are bigger too
  But there's still a place
  In a confined space
  For the likes of me and you.

2 I have had my fill of forepeaks
And I'm sick of engine rooms
And my eyes have cried for mercy
From the sting of welding fumes.
I recall the days of piecework
When I risked my health for gold
  And my only God
  Was a welding rod
  And the job was never cold.

3 When the shipyard gates are opened
And the morning buzzers blow
And the bank is black with workers
All reluctant for to go
You can quickly spot a welder
He's the one who looks like death
  But you mustn't scoff
  When you hear him cough
  And you see him fight for breath.

4 There's just one thing keeps me going
As I fight to keep my health
It's the thought that I might make it
In my quest for worldly wealth.
Just to check my football coupon
And to find a winning line
  That will be my day!
  But till then I'll stay
  Beneath the minus sign.

5 I was born to be a loser
beneath the minus sign
And was doomed to be a welder
In the shipyards of the Tyne.
I have toiled in Hawthorn Leslies
And I've sweated with the best
  I have struggled hard
  In the Naval Yard
  And in Swan's both East and West.

Ripyard Cuddling

The following pages contain many ideas of what to do with the poems in this section. There are opportunities for speaking and writing.

oral work

Here are some suggestions of activities arising from the poems which involve talking, listening, discussing and even performing. Some of these ideas might lead to written assignments, but that is up to you and your teacher.

performing poems

It is always better to hear a poem than just to read it, but some poems are best when performed. To perform a poem in a group, you need to consider the following points:

■ How many 'parts' could you make? How can the poem be divided up into different voices?

■ Think like a performer. How should people say the lines? Are any actions, sound effects or props needed?

■ You will need to rehearse. Should people learn their lines? Everyone will need a copy of the poem so they know which is their part.

If you take all these points into consideration, your poem should come to life.

The following poems are ideal for performance. You will probably find others which work too. A good size for a group is four people. After the performance, get into groups to discuss how it went. Ideas are provided for further discussion on each poem.

■ *The Production Line*   by Bobby Pearce

To start

Each person in the group reads the poem to themselves, then listens to one member of the group reading it out loud. Now work through these points:

1 Decide how you are going to divide the poem. Can any lines be taken as pairs, or are any lines suitable for the group to say altogether?

2 Are there any actions or sounds you could include to help your performance?

3 The lines in the poem have a regular beat or rhythm. What is it? How does it help to put across the boring nature of the men's job? How will you make this clear in your performance?

4 Although the poem describes a boring job, it is not a depressing poem. What is the mood of 'The Production Line', and how will you put this across?

When you have had your discussions and made your decisions, you are ready to start rehearsing.

After the performance

What are the good and bad points about working on a production line in a factory? In some factories, these jobs are done by robots. Is it better to use robots for boring jobs even if this leads to higher unemployment? What jobs could never be done by robots?

■ *'Maintenance Engineer'*   by Sandra Kerr

To start

Each person in the group reads the poem to themselves, then listens to one member of the group reading it out aloud. Now work through these points:

1 Decide how you are going to divide the poem. There's a part for the husband – find his lines, then decide whether the woman is going to be one person or several, depending upon the size of your group.

166

2 Look carefully at the chorus. Will it be performed by one person or the whole group? Why do you think the chorus is repeated so often and should it be said in the same tone each time? If not, how will you bring this out in your performance?

3 The woman's mood changes throughout the poem. Make a list of words (adjectives) which describe those moods and look carefully for where these changes take place. Bring this out in your performance.

4 What does the last line of the last verse mean? How should it be performed?

When you have had your discussions and made your decisions, you are ready to start rehearsing.

After the performance

Do you think 'maintenance engineer' is a fair description of a woman's role as wife and mother? Can you think of any other titles which would fit? The woman points out that not only is she being exploited, but her husband is too. Is she right? In what ways are they both being exploited?

From: Six Poems for Hospital Workers
by Diana Scott

Each person in the group reads the poem to themselves, then listens to one member of the group reading it out loud. Now work through these points:

1 Look up any vocabulary you do not understand.

2 Decide how you are going to divide the poem. There are four verses which describe different jobs in the hospital, but you do not have to have a different person for each verse. It might, for example, be more effective to divide the lines within each verse. Discuss this in your group.

3 Think carefully about the attitude of the poet and the mood of the characters in the poem. Decide what these are for each verse and how you are going to bring them out in your performance.

4 In preparing your performance, you should pay particular attention to the lines in brackets and the two statements in the last line. How should these be performed?

5 Are there any opportunities for actions?

When you have had your discussions and made your decisions, you are ready to start rehearsing.

After the performance

Why do you think the poet chose to write a poem on behalf of these hospital workers? Why does society undervalue them? What other jobs have low status and pay, and why should this be? What jobs are highly paid and regarded? What does this tell us about the society in which we live?

■ *Mo* from *Six Men Monologues*   by Liz Lochhead

To start

Each person in the group reads the poem to themselves, then listens to one member of the group reading it out loud. Now work through these points:

1 Decide how you are going to divide the poem. Which do you think are the boss's actual words and which are Mo's sarcastic comments? The division isn't clear-cut, so discuss this carefully.

2 The reference to 'Kelvinside' (a middle-class area in Glasgow) and the phrase 'wee bitty' identifies the character as Scottish. If your group feels confident enough, try reading the poem in a Scottish accent and see if this adds to its impact.

3 The poem's humour relies on Mo's sarcasm. How will you bring this out to best effect in your performance?

4 Are there any actions you could use to help with your performance?

When you have had your discussions and made your decisions, you are ready to start rehearsing.

After the performance

Although in this country we have equal pay laws, they do not seem to work. Women still earn only 65 per cent of a man's average wage. What are the reasons for this? Why are the majority of the bosses men? Does it really matter? How could real changes be brought about?

Executive by John Betjeman and
Song of the Wagondriver by B.S. Johnson

This is a performance for two people using two poems. Together, read through the poems and decide which one you will each perform. Discuss how the two poems describe very different men, doing different kinds of jobs, with different lifestyles. By exploring a range of accents, actions and tones, bring out the contrast between the executive and the wagondriver.

After the performance

Which of the two men would you rather be and why? Discuss why certain lifestyles are associated with certain jobs. What is more important – job satisfaction or the amount of money you earn?

other suggestions for oral work

1 Working by yourself or in pairs, choose your favourite poem from this section. How would you present it to the rest of the class? Your task is to give a ten-minute lesson using the poem either by itself or with other materials in a way which will keep the class interested and involved.

2 Give a talk to the class lasting between five and ten minutes on some of the issues raised by the poems, or choose one or two from the following:

■ A Saturday or evening job you do.

■ Jobs done by friends or members of your family.

■ The job you hope to do in the future; information about it and reasons for your choice.

■ A description of an ideal job.

3 Imagine your group has been asked by the Careers Department to choose just five poems from this section for a display to represent the world of work and what it means for your year. You must have good reasons for your choice and be prepared to justify them to the rest of the class. By the end of the discussion the whole class should be able to agree on one list of five poems.

4 Role Play

The following suggestions for role play are for pairs or small groups. The ideas in the poems will help you to get started and then it's over to you.

Labour Exchange by Clifford Dyment

Role play a conversation the men in a Labour Exchange might have about the stresses and strains of being unemployed.

From: Six Poems for Hospital Workers by Diana Scott

Imagine you are the Sociology student and you are going to talk to the hospital orderly and a nurse to get information for your dissertation. (A dissertation is a long and detailed essay that students must complete to get their degree.)
Role play these two interviews, trying to bring out, in particular, how these people feel about their jobs.

Weekend Glory by Maya Angelou

In the poem, the woman tells how she goes to a friend's house on a Saturday night and they plan how to spend their hard-earned evening out. Role play this conversation using clues from the poem.

Woman Enough by Erica Jong

The woman in the poem refers to several other characters; her grandmother, her mother and the man she loves. Choose one or two of these characters and role play the conversation she might have with them. It is likely that any conversation will include a discussion of her job and how she keeps her house.

5   Jobs for Jupiter

This assignment can be for a group or the whole class. You are on a space ship bound for Jupiter. Fuel is running low, and the only way the space ship will reach its destination is if you offload some weight. All non-essential equipment has already gone – it's now down to people. Amongst the passengers are the following:

a teacher   a mechanic
a doctor   a politician
an entertainer   a carpenter
a scientist   a tailor
a nurse   a cook.

(If the whole class is involved, you'll have to add more occupations.) Every member of the group/class takes on the identity of one of the above and has to argue for their importance and therefore survival. Whatever size your group, you have to remove half of its members.

6

This oral assignment involves some advance planning by the teacher and includes opportunities for whole class participation.

a Class or group discussion on how a candidate should present themselves in a job interview.

b The teacher hands out a prepared description of a job vacancy for everyone to read.

c The class divides into groups of up to five members, then decides who will be the candidate and who will be members of the interview panel.

d Candidates leave the group to sit in a 'waiting area' where the teacher will hand them an envelope containing details of the character they will role play. Each candidate will have a different identity with different background details and personality, which they will have to read carefully and think about.

e Meanwhile, within each group, panel members need to decide on the questions they will ask and who will put them. They will probably need to rehearse these.

f All candidates are called to their groups to role play their interview. Groups may be given the opportunity to practise these interviews a couple of times.

g Each group performs their role play for the whole class to watch.

h Either back in groups, or as a whole class, pupils discuss which of the candidates should get the job and which group's panel asked the most suitable questions.

written work

The written work has been divided into two sections: Language assignments and Literature assignments. Within each section, there are opportunities to write in a variety of ways about the poems you have read. The range of written work is designed to meet the requirements of whichever GCSE examination course you are doing. Your teacher will help you to select the right assignments for you and your course.

language assignments

1 Many thought-provoking issues are raised by the poems in this section. This assignment gives you the opportunity to say what you think about some of them. Though individual poems could act as a starting point, it is up to you to do some research on your chosen topic before you begin your final essay. This could take the form of interviewing a range of people who could provide facts and opinions; checking a variety of newspapers for recent stories and using your school and local libraries. Television and radio programmes can also be a useful source of information. Research is necessary so that your opinions can be supported by facts and examples.

The following are not titles, but areas for research which your teacher will help you to explore in order to form the basis of an assignment. Your own title will grow out of your research.

- Any job is better than no job.

- A woman's job is looking after house and home.

- The crafts and their survival.

- Industry and the environment.

- Working to live or living to work?

- Job expectations in relation to social class.

- Work and leisure: striking the balance.

- You are as important as the job you do.

- Running a career and a family.

- Love or money? Working in the caring services.

2 Creative writing

Choose from the following:

a Class reunion

Write a story or a play using this title about a group of classmates (five or six characters) getting together five years after they have left school. Try to include a range of different jobs and lifestyles for your characters which may give rise to resentment or envy.

b Write a story in which someone breaks into the computer network of a multinational company. Show the chaos which results and how it is resolved.

c Wait till your mother gets home

Write a story about a family in which the parents have reversed their traditional roles. The mother goes out to work and the father looks after the house and children. This arrangement is for a trial period only and by the end of your story the family should have decided how they intend to carry on.

d Unfair dismissal

Write a story or a play about the events leading up to the sacking of an employee, for reasons the rest of the workforce think are unfair. You will need to show both the employee's and the boss's points of view and how the situation is resolved.

3

Choose a title from one of the poems in this section and use it as the starting point for a story.

4

In this assignment you are going to do some research on the job expectations of the pupils in your year and assess how realistic they are.

a From a survey of between fifteen and twenty pupils you should explore the following areas:

- How do job expectations differ between boys and girls?

- How much influence do family and friends have on pupils' choices and expectations?

- Which job areas are most popular and why?

- Are expectations linked to local job availability?

In order to gain all this information, you will probably need to devise at least five questions to ask pupils. Think very carefully about how these questions should be phrased.

The first part of your assignment will be the copy of the survey sheet.

b Presenting your findings

The second part of your assignment will be the conclusions of your survey. These should be presented in a variety of ways, e.g. bar graphs, pie charts etc., and will also include written work on the four areas outlined in **a**. You are expected to include comments on your findings.

c Interview stage

Your aim is to choose a particular job and interview a pupil who hopes to do it and an adult already doing it. You will have to be realistic about this. First, find an adult willing to be interviewed, then find a pupil from your survey who wants to do that job.

The following questions are recommended for both interviews:

■ What does the job involve on a day to day basis?

■ Why do you want to/why do you do this job?

■ What training is/was needed?

■ What are the opportunities for promotion?

■ In which ways is this job satisfying/frustrating?

As the interviews will be needed for the next part of the assignment, it is advisable to tape them.

d *Either*: Write down both your interviews. Follow this with a short paragraph commenting on how realistic the pupil's views of the job were.

Or: Write a detailed account comparing and contrasting the pupil's expectations with the reality of the job itself. This should be followed by a more general examination of what schools can do to help prepare pupils for the world of work.

5 Personal writing

Choose from the following:

a Me, my family and work

Write about the jobs the members of your family do and how they feel about them. Include details of any interesting or amusing things that have happened to them at work. Finish off the piece with a description of the job you hope to do and how you think you will adapt to the world of work.

b Work experience

Write about any experiences you have had in the world of work. This could include baby-sitting, a Saturday/evening job, school work shadowing or work experience etc. This should not be limited to an account of what you do, but should include descriptions of people and incidents.

6 Every day, you come into contact with people who are working to make your day run smoothly, e.g. transport workers, shop keepers, teachers. There are also thousands of other employees working to provide the services you take for granted.
Write about a working day in the life of three of these people, which should describe what they do and how they feel about it.

literature assignments

1 What general picture of work emerges from the poems in this section? With close reference to at least five poems, demonstrate what you have learnt about: different working environments, lifestyles associated with different jobs and the benefits and disadvantages of working. Did you learn anything that surprised you?

2 We usually consider 'work' as an activity for which people get paid. Show how some of the poems in this section challenge this belief and also how some of the poets arouse our sympathy for those who work for low wages. You should refer closely to two or three poems, but you may include others if you wish.

3 Choose two poems from this section – one you liked and one you didn't. Write a letter to each of the poets explaining in detail the reasons for your response. Justify your comments by referring closely to each of the poems. Each letter should cover at least a side and a half of A4 paper.

4 Many of the poems in this section are either written by women or about women. With close reference to at least three poems, show how women are represented as feeling about the world of work and their position in it.

5 Choose three to five poems from this section and say why you liked them.

6 Feminine Advice by Liz Lochhead

There are four parts to this assignment.

a Look carefully at verse 2. In what ways is the girl in the poem discouraged from finding herself that 'Good Career' her mother mentions in verse 1? What are your views on the advice she is given in this verse?

b Her mother, her school and the women's magazines all suggest that her eventual 'Good Career' will be to keep her husband happy. What advice do they give her to help her prepare for this position? What are your views on the usefulness of this advice?

c Look carefully at what her mother and the Careers mistress say to her. What does it tell you about the sort of lives they have led? How in their different ways do they have the girl's best interests at heart?

d *Either*: There is another verse to this poem which has been omitted. In it, the poet reveals what life has actually taught her and how the advice she was given was false. The verse begins: 'But I'm aware and now I know that . . .' Finish the verse by adding 15 to 20 lines.
Or: Write your own rap about the advice you have been given by parents, teachers and magazines.
Or: Write a rap called 'Male Advice'.

7 From: Six Poems for Hospital Workers by Diana Scott

There are three parts to this assignment:

a You are a journalist and your paper is running a series of articles about low-paid workers. You are asked to visit the local hospital to interview an orderly, a nurse and a cleaner. Using the information in the poem, write the article, including details about what they do and how they feel about it.
Present your article as it would appear in the newspaper – in columns with a headline and sub-headings. Include quotations from the characters you've interviewed. Your article should cover at least one side of A4 paper.

b Pick out five phrases from the poem which had most effect on you. Give reasons for each choice and explain what the effects were.

c Look at the poem 'Production Line'. What are the similarities and differences between the two poems? Which poem makes its point most effectively and why? You should aim to cover at least a side of A4 paper.

8 Read the following four poems carefully: 'Weekend Glory', 'Vital', 'Executive' and 'Maintenance Engineer'.

What are the views and lifestyles of the four central characters? Imagine they have been brought together for a television or radio discussion programme on *What Work Means to Me*.

In this assignment, you will set out the discussion in play form, giving each character the opportunity to express their views, which must be closely linked to the poems. You will need a chairperson whose job it is to introduce the characters, provide a brief outline of their jobs and ensure that the discussion runs smoothly. It is probably a good idea to provide names for each character.

9   Situations vacant

To complete this assignment, get hold of a situations vacant page from a newspaper so you can study how job advertisements are set out and worded.

a You are going to design your own situations vacant page. In order to do this, select at least five poems from this section which are about particular jobs, paid and unpaid. Take the relevant information from the poems to create advertisements which make those jobs sound attractive. Look closely at the techniques used in your newspaper to help you.

b Select *three* of the jobs from your situations vacant page. The people leaving these jobs have decided to write a true account of what their jobs were like for the person who will replace them. With very close reference to the information, ideas and opinions in the poems concerned, write those three accounts. You may wish to make it clear that the reality of the job is very different from the impression given in the advertisement.

10   The Wife's Tale and Thatcher by Seamus Heaney

The Wife's Tale

In this poem, Heaney describes a peaceful country scene. The couple are obviously close, and take pride in each other's work. The use of figurative language and sense imagery in the poem convey both Heaney's and the characters' affinity with the land.

Support this interpretation of 'The Wife's Tale' by close reference to the poem.

Thatcher

Read 'Thatcher', which is also by Heaney. What evidence is there that the two poems were written by the same poet? You should refer in particular to subject matter, tone, diction and use of figurative language.

11 Weekend Glory by Maya Angelou and Labour Exchange by Clifford Dyment

In their different ways, these poems focus on what people do when they're not working. In 'Weekend Glory', the woman's free time is a cause for celebration, whereas for the men in 'Labour Exchange', it is a burden. By careful study of each poem, show how the poets have achieved these contrasting effects.

12 Elegy for Alfred Hubbard by Tony Connor

a During Alfred Hubbard's funeral service, the Vicar of St Mark's Church would make a speech in commemoration of Hubbard's life and work. Write that speech, carefully selecting what you consider to be the relevant details from the poem.

b After a funeral service, families usually hold a wake (a social gathering for friends and relatives). Write the conversation in play form you think two or three of Hubbard's friends or neighbours might have about the sort of man he really was.

In both these tasks, you should be sensitive to the affectionate tone used throughout the poem.

13 'Maintenance Engineer' by Sandra Kerr, Woman Enough by Erica Jong and Mo by Liz Lochhead

At the end of the poem 'Woman Enough' Erica Jong writes:

'. . . after all these centuries
it is easier for him
than for me.'

Show how the truth of this statement is demonstrated in all three poems and the differing responses to it.

14 Executive by John Betjeman and Vital by Alan Brownjohn

The men in both these poems have responsible jobs in middle management. While one is thriving on the status and power of his position, the other is finding the pressure unbearable. With close reference to the poems, try to explain why they respond differently. You should consider how the poets have represented the personalities, home lives, social class and ambitions of the two men.

15　Cleator Moor by Norman Nicholson and Book of Stones by Robert Morgan

Cleator Moor

In the first part of this assignment, you are going to do a detailed annotation (critical and explanatory notes) of the poem. In order to do this, you will need to copy the poem out in three sections – verses 1 to 3, 4 and 5, 6 to 8. Each section should be well spaced out on a separate sheet of A4 paper.

Your task is to work through the poem, looking for and commenting on examples of the following:

- Industrial/agricultural images.

- Choice of verbs.

- The theme of exploitation of the land and its people.

- The contrast between poverty and plenty.

- The relationship of Cleator Moor to the outside world.

- The structure of the poem.

- How the poet conveys his attitude to all of the above.

Make your points by underlining the relevant words or phrases and writing your comments nearby in the spaces you have left around each verse.

Book of Stones

Read 'Book of Stones' and write a detailed comparison of the two poems.

16　Elegy on a Tyneside Shipyard by Ripyard Cuddling

This poem has been printed with the verses in the wrong order. Your task, with a partner or in a small group, is to rearrange the verses and put them in an order or sequence that makes sense.

First, decide which verse you would use to start the poem. Now you can begin sequencing the rest of the poem. You don't necessarily have to work through in order – you could, for example, agree on which verse ends the poem and position that before you have rearranged the middle.

Although the verses have been numbered and you could decide on an order using only the numbers, the easiest way to complete this exercise is to copy the poem and cut it out so you can move the verses around. Using this method, you can try various combinations. Remember, since one of your written tasks will be to write an account of this process, it is a good idea to take notes at this stage.

When you have decided on your order, stick down the completed version on a sheet of paper (each of you will need a copy for your written work). Compare your findings with that of other groups and check with your teacher before you begin to write. (We have not included the correct version here because we are confident you will be able to work it out for yourselves.)

When you have completed your sequencing of the poem, there are three written tasks to undertake:

a Write a detailed account of the sequencing process, explaining exactly how you arrived at your final version.

b The dictionary defines an elegy as 'a song of mourning after loss'. In this poem, what losses are being mourned by the poet? Refer in close detail to the language in the poem which helps to build the elegiac effect.

c Write the letter you think this welder might send to a national newspaper outlining his feelings about the working conditions in a Tyneside shipyard.

Waiting for the bell

We have included a selection of poems about schools, pupils and teachers because we know you're all experts on the subject. You might feel that school is rather like a life sentence at the moment, but love it or hate it, we hope you'll find some poems here which express your feelings. If you read on, you might even learn a surprising thing or two about what your teachers think . . .

■ *Starting School*

Of all the milestones in this life
The one I've found most cruel
Is that traumatic, awful day
When first we go to school.
I still remember how I felt
So full of little fears,
Yet trying hard to look at ease
While forcing back the tears.
For, all at once, a strange new world
Was waiting to be known,
I turned around, but mam was gone
And I was on MY OWN!
A fat girl with a yellow fringe
Was bawling loud and long,
I stood there in my wellingtons
Determined to be strong.
Then teacher took my sweaty hand
And led me to my seat;
'Now, what's your name?' she gently said –
I stared down at my feet.
My mouth was dry, my stomach churned
I seemed to lose my voice
Then out it came in one long squeak,
'Please Miss – my name is Joyce'.
Then all the children sang a song,
I felt my spirits rise
And everything was somehow changed
Before my very eyes.
'Miss' drew a picture, all in chalk,
We played some lovely games
And long before the dinner bell
I'd learned the children's names.
I ate my lunch – cold toast it was,
Washed down with cold sweet tea –
The fat girl with the yellow fringe
Was bawling still:

'Dear me what babies some girls are,' I thought,
I'm glad I didn't cry,
'Well, school's all right,' I said to mam.
She smiled – I wonder why?

Joyce Latham

Late

You're late, said miss.
The bell has gone,
dinner numbers done
and work begun.

What have you got to say for yourself?

Well, it's like this, miss.
Me mum was sick,
me dad fell down the stairs,
the wheel fell off me bike
and then we lost our Billy's snake
behind the kitchen chairs. Earache
struck down me grampy, me gran
took quite a funny turn.
Then on the way I met this man
whose dog attacked me shin –
look, miss, you can see the blood
it doesn't look too good,
does it?

Yes, yes, sit down –
and next time say you're sorry
for disturbing all the class.
Now get on with your story,
fast!

Please miss, I've got nothing to write about.

Judith Nicholls

183

First Day at School

A millionbillionwillion miles from home
Waiting for the bell to go. (To go where?)
Why are they all so big, other children?
So noisy? So much at home they
must have been born in uniform
Lived all their lives in playgrounds
Spent the years inventing games
that don't let me in. Games
that are rough, that swallow you up.

And the railings.
All around, the railings.
Are they to keep out wolves and monsters?
Things that carry off and eat children?
Things you don't take sweets from?
Perhaps they're to stop us getting out
Running away from the lessins. Lessin.
What does a lessin look like?
Sounds small and slimy.
They keep them in glassrooms.
Whole rooms made out of glass. Imagine.

I wish I could remember my name
Mummy said it would come in useful.
Like wellies. When there's puddles.
Lellowwellies. I wish she was here.
I think my name is sewn on somewhere
Perhaps the teacher will read it for me.
Tea-cher. The one who makes the tea.

Roger McGough

The Class

Quite often
you sit with your back to the teacher
you bounce a ping-pong ball on the table
you practise breaking your mate's neck
you beat rhythms on his back
you sit on top of the cupboard
you climb out of the window

Sometimes
you notice there's a teacher in the room
and he or she says,
'Now I would like you to do this . . .'
Then you throw a ball of paper at the wall
you yell your mate's name three times
you break your mate's pencil up
you stick the broken pencil in your mate's ear
you throw your mate's pen in the bin
you try smacking the top of your head
   and rubbing your belly at the same time
you fall off your chair
you say,
'If frozen water is called iced water
   what do you call frozen ink?'
'Er . . . iced ink?'
'Ugh . . . YOU STINK!'
You say:
'Humpty Dumpty sat on the wall
Humpty Dumpty had a great fall
All the king's horses
and all the king's men
trod on him'

The teacher seems to be talking too.
The teacher seems to be talking to you.
The teacher says,
'I've told you what to do – so do it.'
So you say,
'What do you want us to do now sir?'

So you climb into the cupboard
you climb out of the cupboard
you jam a table into your mate's belly
you nick your mate's bag
you eat his crisps
you say, 'Get lost, earoles.'
The teacher seems to be saying to you,
'Hey. You. Sit on your own.'

So you make Match of the Day noises
you wave your arms in the air
you sing, 'Come on you re-eds
          'Come on you re-eds'
you say, 'If you were living in a bungalow
and you painted the bedroom red,
the bathroom white,
what colour would you paint the stairs?'
'I dunno – blue?'
'No. There aren't any stairs, it's a bungalow.'
You say,
'Knock knock'
'Who's there?'
'Cows.'
'Cows who?'
'No they don't. Cows moo.'
So you bend your mate's ruler backwards
and forwards
and backwards.
It breaks.
The teacher seems to be saying to you,
'Report to the Head!'
and you say,
'Why?
That's not fair,
why pick on me,
what was I doing?'

Michael Rosen

Arithmetic is where numbers fly like pigeons in and
   out of your head.
Arithmetic tells you how many you lose or win if you
   know how many you had before you lost or won.
Arithmetic is seven eleven all good children go to
   heaven – or five six bundle of sticks.
Arithmetic is numbers you squeeze from your head to
   your hand to your pencil to your paper till you get
   the answer.
Arithmetic is where the answer is right and everything is nice and you can look out of the window and
   see the blue sky – or the answer is wrong and you
   have to start all over again and try again and see
   how it comes out this time.
If you take a number and double it and double it again
   and then double it a few more times, the number gets
   bigger and bigger and goes higher and higher and
   only arithmetic can tell you what the number is when
   you decide to quit doubling.
Arithmetic is where you have to multiply – and you
   carry the multiplication table in your head and hope
   you won't lose it.
If you have two animal crackers, one good and one bad,
   and you eat one and a striped zebra with streaks
   all over him eats the other, how many animal
   crackers will you have if somebody offers you five
   six seven and you say No no no and you say Nay nay
   nay and you say Nix nix nix?
If you ask your mother for one fried egg for breakfast and she gives you two fried eggs and you eat
   both of them, who is better in arithmetic, you or
   your mother?

Carl Sandburg

189

■ *Exercise Book*

Two and two four
four and four eight
eight and eight sixteen . . .
Once again! says the master
Two and two four
four and four eight
eight and eight sixteen.
But look! the lyre-bird
high on the wing
the child sees it
the child hears it
the child calls it.
Save me
play with me
bird!
So the bird alights
and plays with the child
Two and two four . . .
Once again! says the master
and the child plays
and the bird plays too . . .
Four and four eight
eight and eight sixteen
and twice sixteen makes what?
Twice sixteen makes nothing
least of all thirty-two
anyhow
and off they go.

For the child has hidden
the bird in his desk
and all the children
hear its song
and all the children
hear the music
and eight and eight in their turn
off they go
and four and four and two and two
in their turn fade away
and one and one make neither one nor two
but one by one off they go.
And the lyre-bird sings
and the child sings
and the master shouts
When you've quite finished playing the fool!
But all the children
are listening to the music
and the walls of the classroom
quietly crumble.
The windowpanes turn
once more to sand
the ink is sea
the desk is trees
the chalk is cliffs
and the quill pen
a bird again.

Jacques Prévert (translated by Paul Dehn) ▨

Truant

Sing a song of sunlight
My pocket's full of sky –
A starling's egg for April,
Jay's feather for July;
And here's a thorn bush three bags full
Of drift-white wool.

They call him a dunce, and yet he can discern
Each mouse-brown bird,
And call its name and whistle back its call,
And spy among the fern
Delicate movement of a furred
Fugitive creature hiding from the day.
Discovered secrets magnify his play
Into a vocation.

Laughing at education,
He knows where the redshank hides her nest, perceives
A reed-patch tremble when a coot lays siege
To water territory.
Nothing escapes his eye:
A ladybird
Slides like a blood-drop down a spear of grass;
The sapphire sparkle of a dragon fly
Redeems a waste of weeds.
Collecting acorns, telling the beads of the year
On yew tree berries, his mind's too full for speech

Back in the classroom he can never find
Answers to dusty questions, yet could teach,
Deeper than blackboard knowledge,
Geometry of twigs
Scratched on a sunlit wall;
History in stones, and seasons
Told by the fields' calendar –
Living languages of Spring and Fall.

Phoebe Hesketh

The Bully Asleep

One afternoon, when grassy
Scents through the classroom crept,
Bill Craddock laid his head
Down on his desk, and slept.

The children came round him;
Jimmy, Roger, and Jane;
They lifted his head timidly
And let it sink again.

'Look, he's gone sound asleep, Miss,'
Said Jimmy Adair;
'He stays up all the night, you see;
His mother doesn't care.'

'Stand away from him, children.'
Miss Andrews stooped to see.
'Yes, he's asleep; go on
With your writing, and let him be.'

'Now's a good chance!' whispered Jimmy;
And he snatched Bill's pen and hid it.
'Kick him under the desk, hard;
He won't know who did it.

Fill all his pockets with rubbish —
Paper, apple-cores, chalk.'
So they plotted, while Jane
Sat wide-eyed at their talk.

Not caring, not hearing
Bill Craddock he slept on;
Lips parted, eyes closed —
Their cruelty gone.

'Stick him with pins!' muttered Roger.
'Ink down his neck!' said Jim.
But Jane, tearful and foolish,
Wanted to comfort him.

John Walsh ▓

194

▪ *Back in the Playground Blues*

Dreamed I was in a school playground I was about
  four feet high
Yes dreamed I was back in the playground and
  standing about four feet high
The playground was three miles long and the playground
  was five miles wide.

It was broken black tarmac with a high wire fence all
  around
Broken black dusty tarmac with a high fence running
  all around
And it had a special name to it, they called it
  The Killing Ground

Got a mother and a father they're a thousand miles away
The Rulers of the Killing Ground are coming out to play
Everyone thinking: who they going to play with today

You get it for being Jewish
Get it for being black
Get it for being chicken
Get it for fighting back
You get it for being big and fat
Get it for being small
Oh those who get it get it and get it
For any damn thing at all

Sometimes they take a beetle tear off its six legs one by one
Beetle on its black back rocking in the lunchtime sun
But a beetle can't beg for mercy, a beetle's not half the fun

Heard a deep voice talking, it had that iceberg sound
'It prepares them for a life' – but I have never found
Any place in my life that's worse than The Killing Ground

Adrian Mitchell ▪

The Lesson

A poem that raises the question:
Should there be capital punishment in schools?

Chaos ruled OK in the classroom
as bravely the teacher walked in
the nooligans ignored him
his voice was lost in the din

'The theme for today is violence
and homework will be set
I'm going to teach you a lesson
one that you'll never forget'

He picked on a boy who was shouting
and throttled him then and there
then garotted the girl behind him
(the one with grotty hair)

Then sword in hand he hacked his way
between the chattering rows
'First come, first severed' he declared
'fingers, feet, or toes'

He threw the sword at a latecomer
it struck with deadly aim
then pulling out a shotgun
he continued with his game

The first blast cleared the backrow
(where those who skive hang out)
they collapsed like rubber dinghies
when the plug's pulled out

'Please may I leave the room sir?'
a trembling vandal enquired
'Of course you may' said the teacher
put the gun to his temple and fired

The Head popped a head round the doorway
to see why a din was being made
nodded understandingly
then tossed in a grenade

And when the ammo was well spent
with blood on every chair
Silence shuffled forward
with its hands up in the air

The teacher surveyed the carnage
the dying and the dead
He waggled a finger severely
'Now let that be a lesson' he said

Roger McGough ▧

Last Lesson of the Afternoon

When will the bell ring, and end this weariness?
How long have they tugged the leash, and strained apart
My pack of unruly hounds! I cannot start
Them again on a quarry of knowledge they hate to hunt,
I can haul them and urge them no more.

No longer now can I endure the brunt
Of the books that lie out on the desks; a full threescore
Of several insults of blotted pages, and scrawl
Of slovenly work that they have offered me.
I am sick, and what on earth is the good of it all?
What good to them or me, I cannot see!

                    So, shall I take
My last dear fuel of life to heap on my soul
And kindle my will to a flame that shall consume
Their dross of indifference; and take the toll
Of their insults in punishment? – I will not! –

I will not waste my soul and my strength for this.
What do I care for all that they do amiss!
What is the point of this teaching of mine, and of this
Learning of theirs? It all goes down the same abyss.

What does it matter to me, if they can write
A description of a dog, or if they can't?
What is the point? To us both, it is all my aunt!
And yet I'm supposed to care, with all my might.

I do not, and will not; they won't and they don't; and
    that's all!
I shall keep my strength for myself; they can keep theirs
    as well.
Why should we beat our heads against the wall
Of each other? I shall sit and wait for the bell.

D. H. Lawrence

History Lesson

Poised on his dusty pedagogic dais,
'Your history prep,' he said 'is a disgrace' . . .
But no surprise showed in a face.

'So, after class, you'll all stay in to con
'That chapter of our set book – Meiklejohn
'On the British Constitution'.

'But, *please*, sir' Cromwell junior starts to fuss,
'What's British history got to do with *us*?'
(Some murmur of a *sotto voce* cuss . . .)

'You'll soon find out, you cheeky young baboon . . .
'Just fail your School Certificate next June,
'Then you'll pipe another tune!'

(Ten-sixty-six to fourteen-eighty-five . . .
For me the period dates alone survive
Of all that immemorial jive.)

Where are they now, who formed that College class?
. . . *Mirabile dictu* . . . so it came to pass
That Cromwell failed, and left at Michaelmas,

Who now, a diplomat, at fifty-three,
Has 'made it' . . . with a (Civ. Div.) O. B. E.,
Or, as they say, 'made history'.

Vivian Virtue

199

Evidence

It was History, Thursday afternoon.

Sometimes what she said made no sense
but she told them in a clear voice
how once riding a bicycle in 1910
they had been pelted from a market stall;
a tomato splattered her white blouse
made and pressed the night before,
little frills running down the front
ruined.

She was so old you couldn't tell:
hands long since bent, face annealed, carved,
white hair frizzed from a perm
and almost a bald patch when she bent her head.

And how in 1912 in the dead of night,
she had stuffed oily rags
into a postbox in the Strand
and set light to it to get the vote.

She skipped about and went beyond the syllabus,
the teacher nervous, sporting a set smile,
the class staring, cautious, nothing to write.

She had sewed for a lifetime
but in the war made shells, drove a bus
(Remember we talked about that,
the teacher said,
how the war made a difference,
seeing how women could work,
and so in 1929 they got the vote)
– made thin green soup in the General Strike
from cabbages thieved before dawn
(You know about the General Strike,
the teacher said,
1926, workers disappointed, led by miners,
brought the country to a halt)
– lost her lover, never married,
met the Jarrow March
(1936, down from the North,
the teacher said,
the unemployed, caused by world recession,
in a long column to protest for work).

And she remembered too
pulling at an arm in the wreckage
of Lyons in Leicester Square
when they bombed it
(1941? the teacher asked,
one of the heavier German raids?)
– the sirens went, but drinking tea,
they couldn't be bothered then
after so many times before.
Fingers pointing straight up and dead.
The arm was her friend.
She remembered that.

There was silence,
except for filing of nails at the back.
The girl stopped, embarrassed,
the class heads down, afraid to unsettle her,
an old frail lady in a chair alone.
(A mistake. It is easier from the books.)

Silence. A quiet nervous laugh.

Her eyes alight,
looking round.
She was disappointed:
You modern girls,
painting each other's nails,
hoping for a man with cars,
and voting, if you did, for Tories.
(The teacher coughed.
We'll bring this to an end.)

He had said to her at the end, 1918,
a lovely gentle man, eyes like a stream,
starting a long death from gas:
We need another one now, the real one,
the war at home.
She had worked for a new world.
When are you girls going to start?

The books were shifted,
the teacher stood,
and thanked on your behalf.

Mike Raleigh

▪ Classroom Politics

They will not forgive us
These girls
Sitting in serried rows
Hungry for attention
Like shelves of unread books,
If we do not
Make the world new for them,
Teach them to walk
Into the possibilities
Of their own becoming,
Confident in their exploring.

They will not forget
If we do not use
Our often-surrendered positions
On the front line
To wage war against
The subtle hordes of male historians
Who constantly edit female experience
And endlessly anthologise
Their own achievements.

They will not accept
The old excuses of their foremothers
If they grow up to find
That we have betrayed them.

Fiona Norris ▪

Percival Mandeville, the Perfect Boy

Percival Mandeville, the perfect boy,
Was all a schoolmaster could wish to see –
Upright and honourable, good at games,
Well-built, blue-eyed; a sense of leadership
Lifted him head and shoulders from the crowd.
His work was good. His written answers, made
In a round, tidy and decided hand,
Pleased the examiners. His open smile
Enchanted others. He could also frown
On anything unsporting, mean or base,
Unworthy of the spirit of the school
And what it stood for. Oh the dreadful hour
When once upon a time he frowned on me!

Just what had happened I cannot recall –
Maybe some bullying in the dormitory;
But well I recollect his warning words:
'I'll fight you, Betjeman, you swine, for that,
Behind the bike shed before morning school.'
So all the previous night I spewed with fear.
I could not box: I greatly dreaded pain.
A recollection of the winding punch
Jack Drayton once delivered, blows and boots
Upon the bum at Highgate Junior School,
All multiplied by x from Mandeville,
Emptied my bladder. Silent in the dorm
I cleaned my teeth and clambered into bed.
Thin seemed pyjamas and inadequate
The regulation blankets once so warm,
'What's up?' 'Oh, nothing.' I expect they knew .

And, in the morning, cornflakes, bread and tea,
Cook's Farm Eggs and a spoon of marmalade,
Which heralded the North and Hillard hours
Of Latin composition, brought the post.
Breakfast and letters! Then it was a flash
Of hope, escape and inspiration came:
Invent a letter of bad news from home.
I hung my head and tried to look as though,
By keeping such a brave stiff upper lip
And just not blubbing, I was noble too.
I sought out Mandeville. 'I say,' I said,
'I'm frightfully sorry I can't fight today.
I've just received some rotten news from home:
My mater's very ill.' No need for more –
His arm was round my shoulder comforting:
'All right, old chap. Of course I understand.'

John Betjeman

■ *Dickens Characters*

They are restless. Their blood flows with anger
And compulsions. Their stern eyes are dark
With confusion. Their growing bones cry out
Against the boundaries of desks and walls.
They tolerate my voice vibrating with education,
But they find no fault with me,
Only what I do for a living.
And what I do must be done according to the law.
They want to join me on the old road
Of knowledge, but they will only stare at shadows,
Lose themselves among the strange turnings,
And hesitate too long at bare places
Trodden by toughs and killers.
Their imaginations are distorted by violence,
Pre-natal interference, cold homes, and by failure
Created by our system which pigeonholes brains
Into grades A, B, and C. I squeeze words hard.
But they lean against them. I squeeze harder,
Trying to reach their personalities and beyond
To the corners of imaginations still bright
With silver thoughts and joys of discovery.
I pause. The silences are places where we can meet,
Or retreat, or hear an inner voice,
Or pray for a second chance with success . . .
'Listen boys . . . the workhouse was a place
Where Oliver was born . . . there were such places
All over England not so long ago . . .
It was a place to go when you were destitute.'
Jackson in the front desk leans forward.

He has free dinners, a prostitute sister,
A neurotic mother and his father is a stranger.
I read a passage on the workhouse boys
And show pictures from my old copy.
They leave their desks and examine the pictures.
Questions are asked and answered and we linger
Over the pictures and wonder. The playtime bells
Ring in the corridors and they leave slowly,
Taking with them vague thoughts of England's
Workhouses and a boy without parents.
Jackson stays behind with the book.
He knows Oliver Twist far better than I.

Robert Morgan

The following pages contain many ideas of what to do with the poems in this section. There are opportunities for speaking and writing.

oral work

Here are some suggestions of activities arising from the poems which involve talking, listening, discussing and even performing. Some of these ideas might lead to written assignments, but that is up to you and your teacher.

performing poems

It is always better to hear a poem than just to read it, but some poems are best when performed. To perform a poem in a group, you need to consider the following points:

■ How many 'parts' could you make? How can the poem be divided up into different voices?

■ Think like a performer. How should people say the lines? Are any actions, sound effects or props needed?

■ You will need to rehearse. Should people learn their lines? Everyone will need a copy of the poem so they know which is their part.

If you take all these points into consideration, your poem should come to life.

The following poems are ideal for performance. You will probably find others which work too. A good size for a group is four people. After the performance, get into groups to discuss how it went. Ideas are provided for further discussion on each poem.

▉ *The Class* *by Michael Rosen*

To start

Each person in the group reads the poem to themselves, then listens to one member of the group reading it out loud. Now work through these points:

1 Do you think the main voice is a boy or a girl? Why? Does it matter?

2 Decide which lines the teacher says.

3 Now look at all the other direct speech in the poem. How can this be divided between the other members of the group?

4 Look at what's left. Who will say this? More than one person? (There's no correct answer, it's up to your group.)

5 Are there any parts which the whole group could say together?

6 Although there is a lot of opportunity to act things out, how much of it do you need to include in your performance?

7 Do you want the rest of the class to be involved in this performance? How? Is it practical?

When you have had your discussions and made your decisions, you are ready to start rehearsing.

After the performance

Discuss how a teacher could have dealt with this class.

▉ *Exercise Book* *by Jacques Prevert*

To start

Each person in the group reads the poem to themselves, then listens to one member of the group reading it out loud. Now work through these points:

1 Decide which lines the teacher says.

2 There are some parts of the poem which can be chanted by the whole group. Look closely for these, they're not all obvious.

3 This poem relies on the repetition of words and phrases. What are they? Look for them all. What effect is the poet trying to create?

4 Think about the bird. Is there really a bird there, or is it just in the children's imaginations? What do you think the bird is supposed to represent in this poem?

5 If one member of your group is the teacher, and you're all involved in chanting the numbers, how do you want to divide what's left into parts for the group? (There is no correct answer, it's up to you.)

6 At the end, the poet imagines

'... the walls of the classroom
quietly crumble.'

Look at the last seven lines and discuss why you think the poem ends in this way.

When you have had your discussions and made your decisions, you are ready to start rehearsing.

After the performance

Think back over your experience of education since you were five. How much time have you been given to think, create and discuss? How was your primary school different from your secondary in the kinds of activities you were expected to do? Are schools too concerned with teaching facts?

The Bully Asleep   by John Walsh

To start

Each person in the group reads the poem to themselves, then listens to one member of the group reading it out loud. Now work through these points:

1 What picture of Bill Craddock do the first four verses conjure up? How are we meant to feel about him at this stage? How are our views changed by the information contained in the second half of the poem?

2 Look at the direct speech in the poem and decide which characters say which lines.

3 How will you divide the rest of the poem?

4 Think very carefully about the volume and pace of your performance. How will it change? Look for clues in the poem which indicate how the lines should be said.

5 After all we learn about Bill Craddock, why does Jane want 'to comfort him' at the end of the poem? How will these last two lines be performed?

6 Are there any actions you could use to help with your performance?

When you have had your discussions and made your decisions, you are ready to start rehearsing.

After the performance

Discuss the way Jimmy and Roger react to the fact that Bill Craddock is asleep in their lesson. Why do they behave this way? Now look at the response of Miss Andrews and Jane. Why is it different? Who do you think is right?
From the clues in the poem, how do you think Bill Craddock behaves when he is awake and how might the four characters respond to him then?

▨ *The Lesson* *by Roger McGough*

To start

Each person in the group reads the poem to themselves, then listens to one member of the group reading it out loud. Now work through these points:

1 What is the difference between capital and corporal punishment?

2 Decide which lines the teacher says.

3 Look at the first two verses of the poem only. What *could* this lesson have been about?

4 Make two lists, one of all the words and phrases you'd expect to find in a poem called 'The Lesson', and the other containing any words and phrases associated with violence.
Now look carefully at how words and phrases from both the lists come together in the poem. Does every verse contain examples from each list? Why do you think the poet did this?

5 Discuss carefully how you want to divide the poem so that your group can perform it.

6 Do you want to involve the whole class in this performance? Remember, if you have too much action, the poem might get lost in the din!

When you have had your discussions and made your decisions, you are ready to start rehearsing.

After the performance

Do you think teachers have fantasies like the one in the poem? What point was Roger McGough trying to make about the job of a teacher when he wrote 'The Lesson'?

▨ *Evidence*   *by Mike Raleigh*

To start

Each person in the group reads the poem to themselves, then listens to one member of the group reading it out loud. Now work through these points.

1 In the poem there are many references to the past. Sort out which are the old lady's memories and which are the facts being supplied by the teacher.

2 From whose point of view is the poem written?

3 Many of the experiences in the old lady's life are very sad, but what *language* does the poet use to arouse our sympathy for her? Pick out particular words and phrases which do this, then contrast them with those used to describe the young girls. How are we meant to feel about them?

4 Why does the line:

'Silence. A quiet nervous laugh.'

stand by itself? How should this line be performed? Are there any other key lines in the poem?

5 Think carefully about how you are going to divide this poem into parts. You might like to distinguish between the old lady's words and her thoughts.

6 If you had to choose one word, line or phrase from the poem as a new title, which would it be?

When you have had your discussions and made your decisions, you are ready to start rehearsing.

After the performance

Is the teacher right in thinking it was: '(A mistake. It is easier from the books.)'?

Back in the Playground Blues   by Adrian Mitchell

To start

Each person in the group reads the poem to themselves, then listens to one member of the group reading it out loud. Now work through these points:

1   Which words in the first two verses suggest that the playground is like a prison exercise yard?

2   The poet calls the playground 'The Killing Ground'. What is meant by this?

3   The section which starts: 'You get it for being Jewish ...' could be said by the whole group together or you could divide it up for individuals. Which do you think works best?

4   Who is the child in the poem afraid of and why?

5   The poem is written in the form of a blues song. Would some background blues music help your performance?

6   Think about how the teacher's line, 'It prepares them for a life', should be said. What is an 'iceberg sound'?

7   When you've discussed all these points, think about the best way to divide this poem.

When you have had your discussions and made your decisions, you are ready to start rehearsing.

After the performance

How serious a problem is bullying in schools? What sort of people are the bullies? What sort of people are their victims? What can be done by pupils and teachers to prevent this problem?

other suggestions for oral work

1   Working by yourself or in pairs, choose your favourite poem from this section. How could you present it to the rest of the class? Your task is to give a ten-minute lesson using the poem either by itself or with other materials, in a way which will keep the class interested and involved.

2   Give a talk to the class lasting between five and ten minutes on some of the educational issues raised by the poems.

3   There are certain phrases which all teachers use, for example, 'I'm talking to you!' Go through the poems and pick out some more. In pairs, make a list of the twenty most common 'catchphrases' used by teachers in your school. After you've decided on your list, make a chart like this:

catchphrase	all teachers use it	some teachers use it	male teachers use it	female teachers use it

Tick the columns most appropriate for each catchphrase, then when you've done all twenty, see if you can draw any conclusions. Report your findings to the rest of the class.

4   Role Play

The following suggestions for role play are for pairs or small groups. The ideas in the poems will help you to get started.

Late or The Class

Imagine you are the teacher from one of these poems talking to a colleague in the staffroom at break. It is important to show the teacher's feelings as well as referring to what happened in the lessons.

The Bully Asleep

Role play a conversation between Miss Andrews and the boys in which she is telling them off for their treatment of Bill Craddock while he was asleep. The boys should try to defend their behaviour.

Evidence

Role play a conversation between two pupils who were in the History lesson – one who enjoyed the talk and one who was bored by it. Each pupil should make clear the reasons for their different responses.

5   Heard it on the news

Your local radio station is planning to make a new programme for young people called *Schools Today*. You have been asked to make a tape to send in. The only information you have been given is that the tape can last up to five minutes and can deal with any educational issues which you feel are important to the pupils in your school. You can concentrate on one topic only or try to cover a range of ideas.

In order to make the tape, you might like to use some of the ideas from the poems, interviews with other pupils or interviews with staff. If it's all talking, however, it might be rather dull, so think about using some appropriate background sound effects, or even some suitable music. Remember that your audience will be the general public, not just other pupils.

This activity can be done individually, in pairs, or in small groups.

6   In pairs or groups:

a Look for evidence (clues) in any of the poems in the section to support the following statements:

Teachers always win in the end.
Education is too concerned with preparing pupils for exams.
Schools are not strict enough.
Teachers can (and should) learn from pupils.
All pupils should stay on at school until they're eighteen.
Teachers get as fed up as pupils.
Many pupils don't want to learn.
Girls do better at school than boys.
Teachers are lazy.
School days are the best days of your life.

Beware – not all these ideas are expressed in the poems.

Record your findings like this:

Statement	Poems which support the statement	How? For example, are there any particular lines you could pick out?

b Discuss whether you think each statement is true or false.

c Is it possible to put these statements in order of priority (importance)? Try it.

d Report your findings to the rest of the class.

■ *written work*

The written work has been divided into two sections: Language assignments and Literature assignments. Within each section, there are opportunities to write in a variety of ways about the poems you have read. The range of written work is designed to meet the requirements of whichever GCSE examination course you are doing. Your teacher will help you to select the right assignments for you and your course.

language assignments

1   An unofficial guide to your school

Many schools have printed handbooks which set out the information needed for new pupils and their parents. This might include details about the uniform, rules, where to go, who does what and other useful items to help pupils settle in. However – how much of it *is* really useful to new pupils? What has been left out?

In this assignment, you are required to produce an *unofficial* school guide that will tell new pupils what it's *really* like in your school. It's probably best to divide your guide up into sections. Here are some suggestions to help you:

The school buildings (descriptions plus a map, showing areas 'safe' from staff).
The facilities (for sports, photography, etc.).
Uniform.
Rules and regulations.
Meals (places to go and places to definitely avoid).
Behaviour/discipline.
Assemblies.
Useful tips.

You can include a section on teachers and lessons, but we recommend you change the names to protect the innocent, the guilty and, most importantly, you!

2   Personal writing

You will have many memories, good and bad, of your years at school. In this assignment you can write about some of these. Below is a list of some titles you might like to choose:

■ First Day (primary or secondary, perhaps contrasting them)

■ Teachers I Have Known

■ Best Day, Worst Day (two contrasting pieces)

■ My Class

■ What I've achieved/If Only (two contrasting pieces: the first invites you to think carefully about what you've achieved at school, not just in lessons, but as an individual and a member of the school community. The second piece asks you to think of how you could have done better all round.)

■ The Secret School Diary Of . . . .

You could use some of the poems as a starting point to jog your memories.

3

Choose *one* of the titles from a poem in the collection, or the title of the collection itself, 'Waiting for the Bell', as a starting point for any essay about school, or a poem of your own.

4

Many educational issues are raised in this collection of poems. This assignment gives you the opportunity to say what you think about some of them. Any of the poems could act as a *starting point*, but it is then up to you to do some research on your chosen topic before you begin your final essay. This could take the form of interviewing staff, school governors, pupils and parents, checking a range of newspapers for recent stories and using the local and school libraries. Television and radio programmes can also be useful sources of information. Research is necessary so your opinions can be supported by facts and examples.

Here are some suggestions of topics you could choose:

School is not always relevant to young people's needs.
Streaming versus mixed ability.
What employers expect of school leavers.
What subjects should be on offer in secondary schools.
Discipline in schools.
Violence in schools.
Bullying.
Corporal punishment in schools.

Teacher morale/pupil morale.
Public versus state schools.
Equal opportunities in relation to race, class and sex.

These are not titles; they are areas for research which your teacher will help you to explore and group together, if necessary, to form the basis for an assignment. Your own title will grow out of your research.

5 Most radio stations give their listeners the opportunity to 'phone in' to express views on current issues. In this assignment, you are going to produce a 'transcript' (a word for word account) of a radio phone in about the state of education today. This transcript will be written in the form of a play. Here is your cast:

■ Programme *host/DJ*.

■ The *panel*: two or three 'experts' on education. Choose from a pupil, a teacher, a parent or a politician.

■ Between three to five *callers* (members of the public ringing up to ask questions or make comments).

Your first task is to decide on the issues your callers will raise. Do some research on these. The poems will give you plenty of ideas. Your play should follow this pattern:

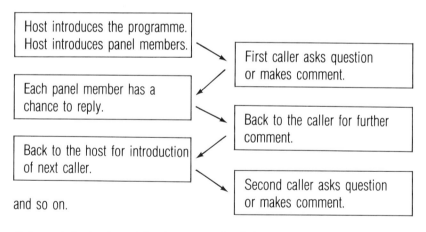

and so on.

At the end, the host must thank everyone for their contributions and make some final comments on what was said.
Make sure that each caller raises a different issue and that your panel members differ in their opinions. Remember that most people (especially experts!) will have a lot to say in a programme of this kind, so try to get a good debate going.

6 The poems in this collection are all written from the point of view of teachers or pupils. Where is the parent's voice?
Write an essay outlining what role parents should play in education today.

7 Select the poem you enjoyed most from this section. Imagine you are able to invite the poet to your school to speak to the pupils about his/her poetry.
For this assignment, you have been given the task of organising the event. This will include:

■ A letter of invitation to the poet explaining why he/she was chosen.

■ A poster advertising the event.

■ A selection of letters to people whose co-operation will be needed, e.g. headteacher, schoolkeeper, other members of staff.

■ A report for the school newspaper describing how the visit went.

8 **a** What makes a good teacher? Write a piece from the point of view of the pupil.

b What makes a good pupil? Write a piece from the point of view of a teacher. You will find plenty of ideas in the poems to get you started.

literature assignments

1 Imagine you are a reporter and you are putting together a section for your newspaper on 'Education Today'.
Choose at least four of the poems in 'Waiting for the Bell' which you enjoyed and felt said something important about schools. You are going to make up interviews with the characters; describe some of the scenes; and write about the issues raised in these poems as the material for your section.
Set it out in columns, like a newspaper, and think carefully about suitable headlines. Include any pictures and captions you wish.
You should aim to cover two to three sides of A4 paper.

2 Do you think this collection of poems represents a realistic view of schools and education? Refer in close detail to at least five poems.

3 Show how the value and worth of education is challenged in this collection of poems. Refer in close detail to at least five poems.

4   Choose up to five poems from this section which you particularly enjoyed and say why you like them.

5   This section contains poems which cover a wide range of educational issues seen from varying points of view. Some of the poems are similar in content and style, so you are asked to choose just ten poems which in your opinion make the most important statements on education but still maintain a balanced overview.

Compile your list of poems, then write a justification of your choice, also explaining why you omitted the others.

6   Choose two poems from this section – one you liked and one you didn't. Write a letter to each of the poets explaining in detail the reasons for your response. Justify your comments by referring closely to each of the poems. Each letter should cover at least one and a half sides of A4 paper.

7   Starting School by Joyce Latham and First Day At School by Roger McGough

a Starting School

Write an essay about this poem. Working through the following points will help you:

- Say what the poem is about and how well it describes a first day at school. Pick out three descriptions you particularly liked and say why.

- What does the word 'traumatic' mean and why do you think the poet chose to use it?

- Pick out and comment on all the clues in the first half of the poem which tell you the girl is frightened when she first arrives at school. How well has the poet conveyed the girl's feelings?

- What are the activities in the second half of the poem which make the girl feel better and why do they have this effect?

- What role does the girl 'with a yellow fringe' have in the poem?

- Explain what the last two lines in the poem mean. Why does 'mam' react in this way?

Your essay should cover about one and a half sides of A4 paper. You should try to link the points together smoothly.

b In what ways are the two poems similar? What do both children worry about? What are the differences between the poems? Write in detail about the descriptions in 'First Day At School'. Say which poem you liked best and why.

You should cover at least one and a half sides of A4 paper.

8 Late by Judith Nicholls and The Class by Michael Rosen

Both these poems, in their different ways, show that it is the pupils who are in charge rather than the teacher. Complete both parts of this assignment.

a What are the situations described in each poem and what methods are the pupils using to disrupt the class? (There are several.) How does each teacher attempt to deal with the disruptive pupils and how successful are they?

b At the end of each poem, the pupils are demanding the teachers' attention in yet another way. Describe what you think happens next in both poems. You can set your work out either as continuations of the poems, in verse form, or in play form.

9 The Class by Michael Rosen

a Imagine you teach the boy described in this poem. You've had enough of his behaviour. Write a letter of complaint to his form tutor.

b Now imagine you are his form tutor and have just received the letter of complaint. You decide to keep him in after school. Give an account of the conversation you have with the boy. Write this in play form.

10

After carefully reading 'The Class' by Michael Rosen, turn this poem into play form. You will need to start with a cast list, so work out how many characters could be speaking in the poem. Next, describe the setting. Stage directions are also very important, since there is a great deal of action in the poem. Remember that directions are always written in the present tense. Try to include details of the characters' expressions and tone of voice as you are writing out the speeches.

Now write a continuation of your play, showing what happens when the boy reports to the Head.

11 Arithmetic by Carl Sandburg

a Describe how the child in the poem tries to make sense of the different aspects of arithmetic. What are the difficulties? How does the child try to overcome them? Refer closely to the details in the poem.

b Write your own poem in the same style as 'Arithmetic'. Choose an aspect of any subject you study at school, e.g. spelling, map reading, experiments, essay writing. Try to make clear all the difficulties that can be encountered and the value of the activity concerned.

12 Arithmetic by Carl Sandburg and Exercise Book by Jacques Prévert

a Show how Carl Sandburg successfully conveys the confusion in the child's mind about the mechanics of Arithmetic. You should refer closely to the definitions and examples he uses; choice of language; structure of the poem; use of humour and the way he evokes our sympathies for the child.

b Compare and contrast 'Arithmetic' and 'Exercise Book'.

13 Exercise Book by Jacques Prévert and Truant by Phoebe Hesketh

How, in their different ways, do both poems highlight the conflict between the world of nature and the world of school? Where do the poets' sympathies lie? Which poet, in your opinion, makes their point best?

14 First Day at School by Roger McGough and Back in the Playground Blues by Adrian Mitchell

Both these poems feature a small child in a primary school playground. While the first poem treats the child's fears in an amusing way, the second creates a far more chilling effect. With close reference to language and style, show how the two poets achieve these contrasting moods.

15 The Lesson by Roger McGough and Last Lesson of the Afternoon by D. H. Lawrence

Both poems are written from the point of view of the teacher. Say what you liked about the poems and why, in their different ways, they are effective.

16 Last Lesson of the Afternoon by D. H. Lawrence

Write a critical appreciation of this poem. Addressing the following points will help you:

■ Who is the poet speaking to in the poem? Who are the questions directed towards? Are they ever answered?

■ What effect is created by likening the pupils to a 'pack of unruly hounds' in the first stanza?

■ In the third stanza, Lawrence refers to 'their dross of indifference'. How does this link up with the description of the pupils' books in the second stanza?

■ Comment on the use of the word 'punishment' at the end of the third stanza.

■ Work through the poem, picking out the words and phrases which:
   a reflect the teacher's weariness, e.g. 'tugged', 'strained'
   b reveal his negative state of mind, e.g. 'I cannot', 'no more'

■ The tone of the poem changes from despair, through anger, to flippancy and then back to anger, and then despair. Carefully trace this development and decide where the transitions are made.

■ Explore the use of punctuation to create pace and tone.

■ Work out the rhyming pattern. How does it contribute to the poem's success?

17

a 'History Lesson' by Vivian Virtue is set in a Jamaican classroom, where the pupils are being prepared for a history examination set by a university in Britain. With close reference to both style and language, show how this poem achieves its ironic effect.

b The teacher in 'Evidence' by Mike Raleigh tries to make history more relevant by inviting an outside speaker into the classroom to share the memories of her early life with the pupils. The ultimate failure of this strategy causes the reader to feel sympathetic towards the old lady and share her annoyance with the young girls. By careful reference to the language of the poem, show how this response is created.

c Establish who or what is to blame for the failure of both these history lessons.

18   Percival Mandeville, the Perfect Boy by John Betjeman

Write a critical appreciation of 'Percival Mandeville'. Addressing the following points will help you:

■ What qualities does Percival Mandeville have which make him a 'perfect boy'?

■ What language highlights the fact that the boys are at a public school?

■ Is there anything in the poem which suggests that Percival Mandeville will become a man with power and status in the future?

■ The description of the night and morning preceding the planned fight is full of references to familiar domestic objects and activities. Why do you think that Betjeman includes these details?

■ Why is it so important that Betjeman should appear 'noble' in the delivery of his excuse?

■ What is it that Percival Mandeville understands at the end of the poem?

■ What is the function of the direct speech in the poem?

■ Is there any humour in the poem? How is it achieved?

19   Dickens Characters by Robert Morgan

For discussion

In groups, read the poem and discuss what points you think the poet is trying to make. Try to identify at least five.
Your written assignment on this poem is to examine the following three areas. You should aim to write at least a side on each.

a   'But they find no fault with me,
     Only what I do for a living'.

     What evidence is there in the poem that the teacher is a good one?

b How does the poet build up a picture of the boys in the class? Look closely at Morgan's choice of words, use of contrast and figurative language.

c From your understanding of 'Dickens Characters' and the issues Morgan raises, which in your opinion are the *three* most important? Support your choice with close reference to the poem.